THE MODERN REEF AQUARIUM
By Dr. C. W. Emmens

Reef aquaria have become rather easy to establish because of the new technology available to hobbyists. Photo by Dr. C. W. Emmens.

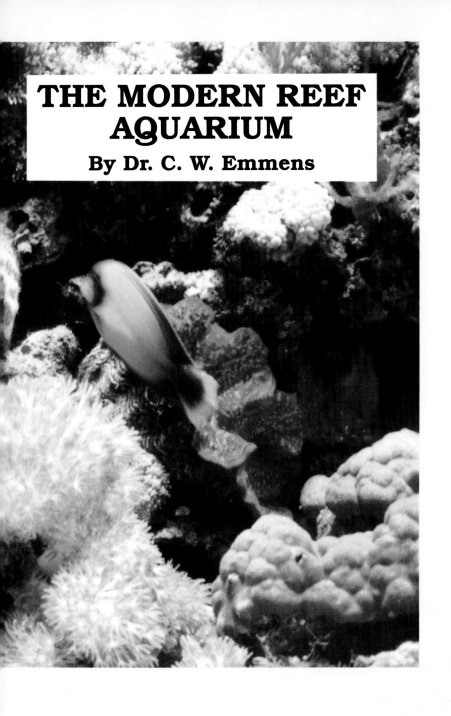

THE MODERN REEF AQUARIUM
By Dr. C. W. Emmens

Distributed in the UNITED STATES to the Pet Trade by T.F.H. Publications, Inc., One T.F.H. Plaza, Neptune City, NJ 07753; distributed in the UNITED STATES to the Bookstore and Library Trade by National Book Network, Inc. 4720 Boston Way, Lanham MD 20706; in CANADA to the Pet Trade by H & L Pet Supplies Inc., 27 Kingston Crescent, Kitchener, Ontario N2B 2T6; Rolf C. Hagen Ltd., 3225 Sartelon Street, Montreal 382 Quebec; in CANADA to the Book Trade by Macmillan of Canada (A Division of Canada Publishing Corporation), 164 Commander Boulevard, Agincourt, Ontario M1S 3C7; in the United Kingdom by T.F.H. Publications, PO Box 15, Waterlooville PO7 6BQ; in AUSTRALIA AND THE SOUTH PACIFIC by T.F.H. (Australia), Pty. Ltd., Box 149, Brookvale 2100 N.S.W., Australia; in NEW ZEALAND by Brooklands Aquarium Ltd. 5 McGiven Drive, New Plymouth, RD1 New Zealand; in Japan by T.F.H. Publications, Japan—Jiro Tsuda, 10-12-3 Ohjidai, Sakura, Chiba 285, Japan; in SOUTH AFRICA by Multipet Pty. Ltd., P.O. Box 35347, Northway, 4065, South Africa. Published by T.F.H. Publications, Inc.
Manufactured in the United States of America by T.F.H. Publications, Inc.

CONTENTS

The author, Dr. C. W. Emmens.

FOREWORD

Dr. Axelrod has invited me to write a new book on reef aquaria—as the miniature reef tank is now usually known. But he doesn't want a long book. That presents a problem. There are quite a number of books that go in great detail into the various forms of equipment now available. Once you start, it is impossible to keep such a book short, so I shall not try. Instead, I am going to tell you how I and those around me manage our reef aquaria as examples of what normally happens. I shall comment on what we don't usually use, without detailed explanations so that you know of its existence. But that's all.

Since I wrote *Miniature Reef Aquarium in Your Home* in 1988 there have been many developments. Some have been in the direction of simplification but most haven't. We have seen a great increase in automation and an increase in the use of test kits and additives of various kinds. We have learned how to keep various invertebrates that used to die very quickly in our tanks. We have also found that some "impossible" fishes survive in reef tanks. Since nearly all other books concentrate on the equipment rather than the living contents, I shall deal with the latter more fully. After all, why do we have an aquarium in the first place?

When reading this book, please remember that the whole subject is still developing. Improvements in ways of doing things will come from many different sources and countries. Improvements in instrumentation will tend to come from large manufacturing countries that have populations big enough to support them. Such countries, outstandingly the USA, can afford to make a great variety of equipment. Others can not and must often import only a small selection from which the aquarist can choose. So you may have to do the best you can with what is available - and sometimes with what you can afford. Luckily, there are still many ways of achieving a good result, even with restricted equipment.

Inert modern materials such as acrylics and other plastics are used to produce non-rusting, safe tanks and equipment for the reef aquarium. Photo courtesy American Acrylic Mfg.

Energy Savers Lighting

AAM

Hang-on over flow pre-filter

Protein skimmer

lack bio edia

Coralife™ air stone

4 sizes of wet/drys stocked custom sizes no problem

State of t System p

CHAPTER 1
The Tank and Lighting

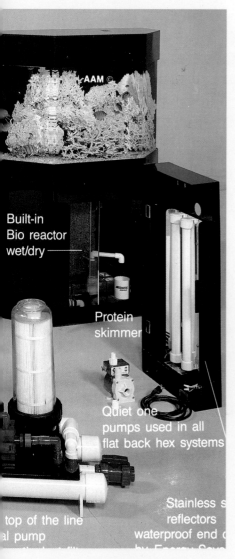

Built-in
Bio reactor
wet/dry

Protein
skimmer

Qdiet one
pumps used in all
flat back hex systems

Stainless s
reflectors
waterproof end

top of the line
al pump

You can have a reef tank of practically any size you like. Small ones obviously restrict the size of corals that you can keep, but can hold a surprising variety of creatures. A reef tank must be crowded if, as we shall see, it is to be self supporting. By that, I mean that you can do without external filtration. However, large tanks enable a much better looking display and allow for growth of the contents. How large, depends on the strength of your floor, the length of your purse and of your arm. Aquaria deeper than about 60 cm (2 ft) are difficult to service because you cannot easily reach the bottom. They also start to become prohibitively expensive.

Reef aquaria are virtually restricted in construction to all-glass or all-acrylic. Older types with metallic frames or with slate or concrete are just too risky as water purity is of first importance. About the only advantage of acrylic is lightness and ease of drilling. Otherwise, it scratches easily and needs to be quite thick in large tanks or it will bow. Certain types are also liable to discolor gradually. So glass is usually the first choice. For the sake of appearance, colorless silicone is preferable, although some authorities believe that a black cement is less likely to leak. The probability of a leak with either is so low that it can be ignored. That is, if the aquarium is really well made—far preferably by a commercial manufacturer. Unless you are highly skilled at the job, don't attempt to make your own tank, it isn't worth it. Most popular designs require drilling a hole in the glass, not for an amateur to attempt.

BASIC PLANS

Few aquarists today prefer the Dutch minireef with which it all started. But the principles upon which it is founded remain in modern versions of the reef tank, although they are beginning to change. The rather noisy set of trays through which overflow water from the aquarium passed has been replaced by other filters. The

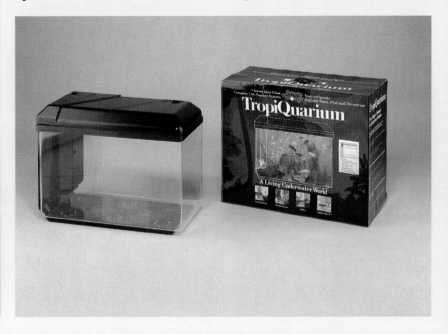

Although tiny tanks are not safe for use as marine aquaria, they can be used as temporary holding tanks and quarantine tanks for invertebrates. Photo courtesy Rolf C. Hagen Corp.

"wet" part of the wet-dry filter is omitted or replaced by a carbon filter. The results are that a modern setup that still retains a trickle filter involves the following:

1. Water flows from the surface of the aquarium into a pre-filter with simple filter padding to catch gross particles. This filter is usually cut off from a back corner of the tank and water flows from it into the trickle filter below. A hole is cut in the base to allow for this. Skimming the surface of the water in the tank removes the film of protein, fatty materials, etc. and allows better gas exchange. Remember that the surface is the window of the tank, where oxygen is absorbed and carbon dioxide is lost. Most reef tanks are left uncovered to increase the availability of fresh air.

2. The trickle filter has either a spray plate or a revolving spray bar to distribute the water evenly over the material below. This may be a double-layered spiral of plastic (DLS), various complexly built balls or other shapes in plastic or

any inert material with a large surface area. It should not trap dirt but should remain of open texture for easy gas exchange. A supply of air may be blown into the base to increase aeration. Bacterial filtration that occurs in the trickle filter uses up lots of oxygen. This makes the filter superior to undergravel filters where the oxygen is extracted from the water in the tank. In the trickle filter, oxygen is supplied by the air and the water remains well oxygenated.

It doesn't much matter which kind of material is used in the trickle filter. All sorts of claims are made for the various types available, but the fact remains that most are perfectly adequate. Why? Because soon after it has been established the living rock in the tank does most of the work. In fact, the trickle filter can be removed in most cases where it has been tried. Nothing happens and the aquarium looks after itself. Perhaps it is less stable than before and an

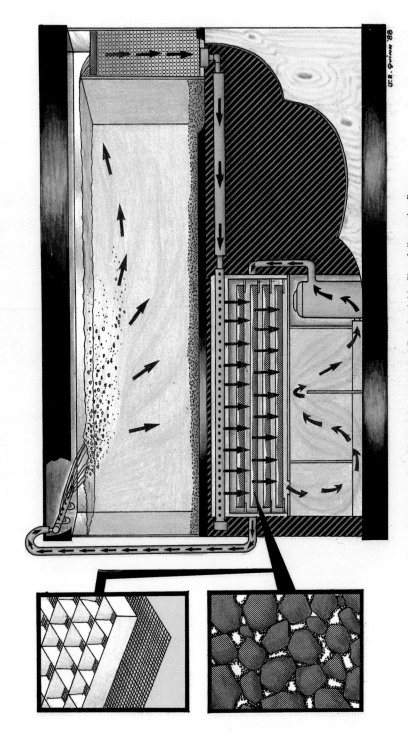

This schematic view of the now outmoded Dutch trickle filter follows the flow of water from the tank through the filter and its trays of biologically active material back to the tank. Art by J. R. Quinn.

13

accidental fouling can more easily cause trouble. Perhaps, but both European and American aquarists are getting away with it without reporting bad results. My own preference is to leave it going since it is already there and if functioning properly it is doing no harm. However, recent investigations indicate that you can start up a reef tank with no trickle filter at all. The pre-filter must remain to skim the surface and remove particular matter. The pump can then return the water as usual.

3. After passing through the trickle filter, water must accumulate in a pump compartment or sump, whence it is returned to the tank. The pump may be submersible or not, but either way a moderate depth of water is required. In order not to clutter up the aquarium, which should look as natural as possible, other equipment can be serviced from or in this sump as well. All kinds of arrangements are made to accommodate carbon filters, protein skimmers, heaters, automatic controls and so on. This means that the sump must be quite large, at least 30cm x 30cm (12" x 12") in plan or be replaced by a series of compartments. The accompanying illustrations make all this

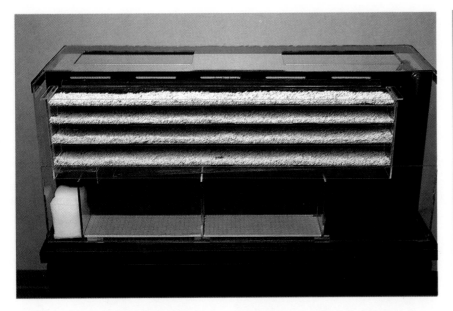

clear. I prefer one large sump that leaves me free to rearrange things as I like.

4. A powerful enough pump is needed to give a water turnover of 3-6 tank volumes per hour. If a single return bar is preferred, it should span the opposite end to the pre-filter just below the water surface. Perforations of suitable size about 2.5cm (1") apart should deliver the returning water along the top of the tank so as to create a turbulent flow. This type of flow causes eddies in the water that swirl it around, changing direction all the time. It can only be achieved with sufficient speed of delivery and care of the level of flow, just under the surface. The result is changing water currents around the corals, etc. and breaking of the water surface. This in turn causes a dappling of the light entering the aquarium, giving a very natural effect.

Some hobbyists like to split the water return so that some is delivered at the base of the aquarium from a bar at the back. The idea is to flush dirt and mulm to the front where it is more easily removed. To achieve this, the reef must not obstruct the flow and must therefore not be built on a solid base, but more about this later.

The reef aquarium is basically a sedentary invertebrate aquarium and can tolerate only a few active animals such as small fishes or shrimp. Photo by Dr. C. W. Emmens.

Canister filters, such as this H.O.T. Magnum 250 from Marineland, are the current rage in aquarium-keeping, providing efficient filtration in a small space and also being easy to maintain. Photo courtesy Marineland.

This arrangement also requires a greater water flow in total or neither spray bar will work satisfactorily. Returns of up to 10 or even 12 tank volumes may be needed. Others like to place water pumps in the tank that may work quite independently of the filtration and main pump. They can then arrange for flow back and forth across the tank, in which case the return water is best delivered only at the base of the aquarium. Equipment is available for timing such independent pumps to give alternate flows at various rates. Alternatively, two return pumps may be used, delivering the water at opposite ends of the tank, with a similar alternate flow.

It may be thought that delivering the water across the top of the tank would result in it heading straight across and down the pre-filter. The water lower down might be left virtually static and unoxygenated. Not so; with or without turbulence, the water sinks as it crosses the tank and sweeps back across the lower regions in a circular flow. It pushes the lower waters ahead of it and together they rise up under the return spray bar to join its current of returning water.

5. It is usual to place the above equipment in a cupboard below the aquarium. There it is out of sight and any noise produced is deadened. The pump must be powerful enough to raise the water up to the top of the aquarium with an adequate flow rate. A non-return valve should be placed in the hose from the pump so that if it fails the water will not be siphoned back and possibly flood the cupboard. Such a valve will only function properly if in an upright position. If the sump is deep enough and only a surface spray bar is used, the valve may be omitted as only a limited back-flow will occur. A float switch may also be fitted to stop the pump from operating if the water in the sump falls too low. The pump is then protected from overheating whether it is submersible or not. Ask your supplier to suggest the most suitable type available.

6. In contrast, the equipment may be placed on the same level as the aquarium. It may be beside

the aquarium, at the back, or even behind a false back divider within the aquarium. Some ingenuity is then required to manage a trickle filter plus all of the rest of the works, but it can be done. The great advantage is that an existing aquarium can be used without having to drill a hole in it. A minor advantage is that a less powerful, cheaper pump will suffice as the water does not have to be lifted. The units

Pressure filter systems are a new approach to the old problem of complete filtration in a small space. Photo courtesy Rainbow Plastics.

21

designed to hang on to the side or back of the aquarium are theoretically less than adequate in size. But the growing practice of relying more on the reef itself to purify the water means that the contribution of the trickle filter doesn't much matter.

LIGHTING

No reef aquarium will succeed unless it receives a great amount of the proper type of lighting. Except for those using the natural system, the lighting to which aquarists are accustomed is quite inadequate. This means that ordinary fluorescent or incandescent lamps are out unless used in profusion. They just do not individually supply enough light and sometimes not the right kind of light.

In the tropics, a flux of light of around 100,000 lux hits the surface of the water at noon. An average of some 50,000 lux during daylight hours would be about right. You can arrange a series of lights to be switched on and off to imitate daily variation, but it is not really necessary. How near to the average flux is needed depends on what you are keeping. Corals found near to the surface of the water may need close to the 50,000 lux mentioned. Those from greater depths do not, because light is absorbed by the water as it penetrates. The flux at 10 meters (33ft) is only around 10,000 lux. It is also different in composition from that at the surface, being nearly all blue-green with practically no red. So there comes the question - what needs this strong light?

The answer to the question is algae. Fishes do not need strong light and many invertebrates do not need it. Crustaceans, echinoderms, most worms and even some soft corals actually shun it. But both macroalgae (fronded plant-like algae) and unicellular algae do need good light. Unicellular algae within the tissues of invertebrates need most light. This is because some is lost as it penetrates the animal's cells before reaching the algae.

CHLOROPHYLL

This is a very special substance shared by all plants and algae. It was invented early in evolution, possibly only once, and has been inherited in very few forms ever since. Chlorophyll has the unique property of absorbing visible light and using the energy gained to manufacture simple sugars, a process known as *photosynthesis*. It is especially dependent on the red and blue ends of the spectrum. Since most macroalgae and many corals flourish best at a depth of around ten meters (33ft) they actually depend on blue

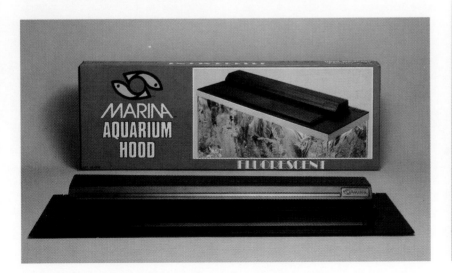

Full but raised hoods help protect the aquarium from airborne contamination, as well as inquisitive pets and people. They also help reduce evaporation, all while providing a place for installing your basic lighting system. Photo courtesy Rolf C. Hagen Corp.

23

light. Above 10 meters there is too much light for many macroalgae that photosynthesize and they grow less well. This may be due to an excess of ultraviolet (UV) light at shallow depths. However, under laboratory conditions, an excess of U V-free light does not increase growth or the oxygen production from photosynthesis.

In using this information to help determine what light intensity is needed in the reef aquarium we must remember the following. Sunlight strikes the water in parallel rays. These lose intensity as they penetrate the water only because of absorption by its contents. A source of light above the aquarium radiates in all directions. Its rays are not parallel, even with a reflector, so that loss of intensity is due to absorption and to spreading. Only a focused beam like a searchlight is anything like sunlight. So we need a greater than otherwise necessary intensity at the surface to get sufficient intensity down below.

If we want 10,000 lux toward the bottom of the aquarium we must supply

Fiber optics is one of the latest additions to tank technology. On the facing page is a tank lighted by actinics with fiber optics serving as a spotlight. On this page are (top) the same tank illuminated by Gro-Lux and fiber optics, contrasted with (bottom) only Gro-Lux. Photos by M. K. Wicksten.

around 50,000 at the top. We shall then have about the same fall-off in light as occurs at 10 meters (33ft) in the ocean. Corals, etc. collected from that depth will get near to what they are used to having, although it will not be shifted so much towards the blue. So will algae, if that matters. In fact, many if not most of our aquarium specimens come from depths of 10-15 meters (33-50ft). Corals from the surface rarely open by day and are not, in general, favored. So we come back to 50,000 lux at the aquarium surface as best imitating nature, even at depths. The effects of this on placement of specimens in a reef tank will be discussed later.

LIGHT QUALITY

To grow land plants in artificial light it is usual to supply both red and blue in excess. Such plants get both in nature. The illumination looks purplish and Gro-lux type fluorescents used over aquaria, giving such light, have been popular because colors tend to be intensified. Gro-Lux fluorescents are not suitable for reef tanks. They

Because of the heat produced, actinic and halide lamps often require special fixtures with cooling fans to operate most efficiently and keep the aquarium temperature within acceptable limits. Photo courtesy Energy Savers.

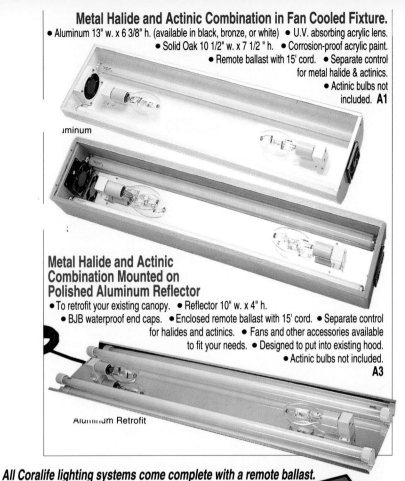

Metal Halide and Actinic Combination in Fan Cooled Fixture.
- Aluminum 13" w. x 6 3/8" h. (available in black, bronze, or white) • U.V. absorbing acrylic lens.
- Solid Oak 10 1/2" w. x 7 1/2 " h. • Corrosion-proof acrylic paint.
- Remote ballast with 15' cord. • Separate control for metal halide & actinics.
- Actinic bulbs not included. **A1**

Aluminum

Metal Halide and Actinic Combination Mounted on Polished Aluminum Reflector
- To retrofit your existing canopy. • Reflector 10" w. x 4" h.
- BJB waterproof end caps. • Enclosed remote ballast with 15' cord. • Separate control for halides and actinics. • Fans and other accessories available to fit your needs. • Designed to put into existing hood. • Actinic bulbs not included.
A3

Aluminum Retrofit

All Coralife lighting systems come complete with a remote ballast.

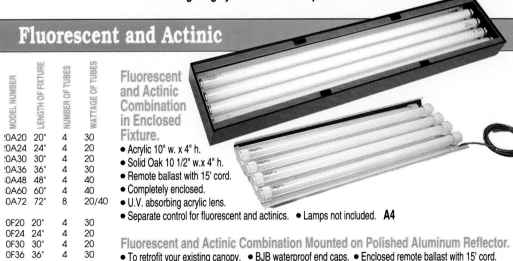

Fluorescent and Actinic

MODEL NUMBER	LENGTH OF FIXTURE	NUMBER OF TUBES	WATTAGE OF TUBES
0A20	20"	4	30
0A24	24"	4	20
0A30	30"	4	20
0A36	36"	4	30
0A48	48"	4	40
0A60	60"	4	40
0A72	72"	8	20/40
0F20	20"	4	30
0F24	24"	4	20
0F30	30"	4	20
0F36	36"	4	30
0F48	48"	4	40
0F60	60"	4	40
0F72	72"	8	20/40

Fluorescent and Actinic Combination in Enclosed Fixture.
- Acrylic 10" w. x 4" h.
- Solid Oak 10 1/2" w.x 4" h.
- Remote ballast with 15' cord.
- Completely enclosed.
- U.V. absorbing acrylic lens.
- Separate control for fluorescent and actinics. • Lamps not included. **A4**

Fluorescent and Actinic Combination Mounted on Polished Aluminum Reflector.
- To retrofit your existing canopy. • BJB waterproof end caps. • Enclosed remote ballast with 15' cord.
- Lamps not included. • Separate control for fluorescent and actinics.
- Fans and other accessories available to fit your needs. **A6**

27

supply insufficient total light per tube and too much red.

Three types of chlorophyll are found in algae, logically enough called a, b and c. Betacarotene is also present in all algae. In addition, brown algae have fucoxanthin and other pigments while red algae have phycoerithrins and phycocyanins. These pigments absorb central spectral and other wavelengths and pass the energy on to chlorophyll. In such algae the whole spectrum may thus contribute to photosynthesis. The energy of the wavelength increases as you pass from red to blue, making the blue end of the spectrum of greatest importance. Why don't plants and algae (which are not typical plants) utilize the ultraviolet? Because it is too powerful, disrupting chemical molecules instead of causing minor changes. The visible spectrum covers the useful range as the infrared is too weak. This is why our eyes see over the same range. They contain pigments that react to light by small changes in structure just like chlorophyll.

The most useful measure of light quality for our purposes is degrees Kelvin (K). It expresses the extent to which a light source emits wavelengths towards the blue end of the spectrum. Sunlight rates 5,000 to 6,000 K, depending on cloud conditions, etc. If we wish to imitate it, that is what to aim for. This is easily achieved with fluorescent tubes that range from about 4,000 (cool white) to 7,500 K (colortones, etc.). So-called daylight tubes are around 6,500 K and very suitable. They give a white light with a good imitation of natural colors as seen in sunlight. Because of different spectral distributions, various makes of tube differ in that regard. Another measure, the color rendition index (CRI), can be used to express how nearly to natural colors appear. Fluorescents range in this index from a CRI of 65-97 or so. In general, the CRI tends to increase with degrees K.

So why don't we use ordinary fluorescent tubes? Because they are too weak and a battery of them is needed. This obstructs the top of the tank, even if enough can be fitted in. A pity, because they are cheap and easy to install. Instead, to get sufficient output we must turn to high output or very high output tubes. These need special ballasts and fittings, do not last very long and are not cheap. So we lose a great deal in

wide a choice to discuss them here.

There is another type of fluorescent tube that has gained considerable attention, the actinic-03 tube. It has a sharp peak of output in the blue, extending regrettably into

turning to them. There are now some "ordinary" fluorescents that do better than previously, so there is hope of a good, cheap source of light after all. Consult your dealer and if necessary an electrician if you choose to try them out. There is too

the ultraviolet. Very little output occurs elsewhere. Not used on its own, but added to other sources of light, it enhances the appearance of a tank if you like a bluish effect. It also helps corals, etc. because of the high blue output.

Because of the U/V output it should not be used without a glass or plastic shield.

METAL HALIDES

There are many light sources other than fluorescents or incandescents. Mercury vapor lamps are too yellow, with a rating of about 3,600 K. Tungsten halogen lamps are no better. Instead, we must turn to metal halides for satisfactory Kelvin ratings. Not all are suitable even then. They are expensive and it is important to choose carefully from those available. Small, plug-in photographic bulbs do not last long. Some pendant-type fittings cannot take bulbs with a high enough Kelvin rating.

The best of the lot is agreed upon by many aquarists as being the Osram HQI Power Star. It is available in various wattages, from 70 upwards. Various Kelvin degrees are offered, from 3,900 K to 5,000 K or more in the higher wattages. Color rendition indices are good, but we need a Kelvin rating of at least 4,300 K for a natural looking light. Power Stars have the great advantage of a long life,

lasting with little spectral change for up to 15,000 hours. Some local manufacturers have licences to make them, issued by Osram. Their specifications may differ from the parent company's product, so be careful to check them with the suppliers.

Some metal halides emit U/V light, so must be shielded by glass in the fitting or over the aquarium. The Power Stars fall into this category. All emit considerable heat, so the preferred pendant types are suspended 30-60cm (1-2 ft) above the tank. This gives a clear tank top, a great advantage. Even with such an arrangement it may be necessary to use a fan to cool the water surface. Naturally, the higher the source of light is placed, the greater the spread of light. The lux reading at the surface therefore falls off, creating a need for a more powerful source. Do not be misled by specifications in lumens, followed by applying the formula, lux = lumens x 10.76. This applies only to emission at the surface of the bulb, not 30-60cm (1-2 ft) away. Minimum requirements for Power

Stars suspended 45 cm (1.5 ft) over a 120cm (4 ft), 300 liter (80 gal) tank would be 2 x 150 watts. Over a 180 cm (6 ft), 450 liter (120 gal) tank use 3 x 150 watts. Lights should be on for a period not much different from 12 hours per day; 10-14 hours are about the limits.

Aquarists often collect "gadgets" of all sorts, from those that are quite useful under certain circumstances, like this U/V sterilizer assembly, to little things that have functions difficult to even guess. Photo by V. Serbin.

Precise digital instruments like the American Marine models shown at right are used by both novice and professional aquarists to monitor conditions in their tanks. Photo courtesy American Marine.

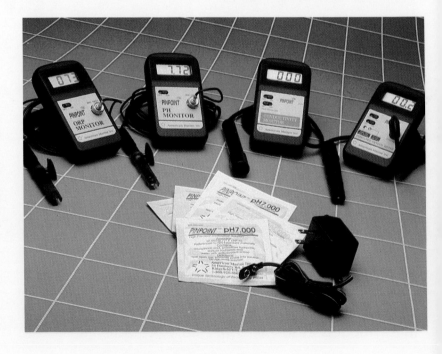

CHAPTER 2
Other Equipment

Here is a list of further equipment you may need for the reef tank. Some of it is virtually essential, but towards the end of the chapter come pieces of equipment that are purely optional or even contraindicated. It is up to you. If you wish to spend a lot of money on gadgetry, go ahead, but remember, the more you install, the more can go wrong.

I have spent some time over lighting because it is of primary importance. We now pass to a topic of almost or perhaps equal importance, although it can be dealt with in shorter space.

PROTEIN SKIMMING

In a protein skimmer or foam fractionator fine bubbles of air are passed through a column of water. Many organic molecules stick to the bubbles since they are attracted to surfaces. The pre-filter skims off those that collect on the water surface, but they are passed on, not

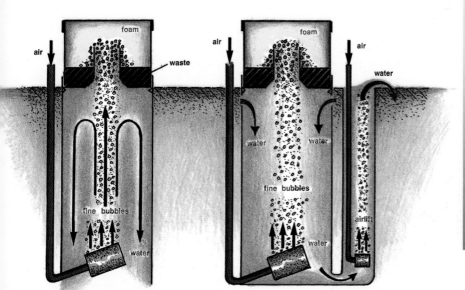

Protein skimmers, also known as foam fractionators and air strippers, remove fine organic molecules by trapping them on the surface of air bubbles.

collected. In a skimmer, the resulting foam is collected in a cup at the top of the column of water. It can then be discarded together with all the muck adhering to it. This consists of proteins, amino acids, phenolic compounds, pigments and other surfactant substances. Ammonia, nitrites and nitrates and such are not collected at the pH of sea water. It would have to be pH 10 or more to do that. If the water is clean, a little light-colored water collects. If it is loaded with pollutants, a smelly dark brown fluid results.

The importance of protein skimming is that it removes matter that would break down into nitrogen-cycle compounds if left. It therefore greatly lowers the load on biological filtration. The longer the air bubbles stay in contact with the water the better it works. So a long upright tube of water with airstones at the base is needed. The relatively simple devices of the past are not good enough. What is needed with a reef aquarium is a counter current model or a Venturi skimmer.

Counter current skimmers use a water pump and an air supply. Aquarium water is pumped in near to the top of the tube, which sits external to the tank. It flows down the tube against the rising bubbles and is returned to the sump or possibly the aquarium. The contact time between them is thus lengthened, increasing efficiency, and the longer the column of water the better. Models from 60cm to 90cm (2-3 ft) high, excluding the cup at the top, are popular. However, even longer contact tubes may be used with advantage. The best airstones for the purpose are wooden ones, which give the finest bubbles but must be renewed rather frequently as they clog up. They are cheap, so don't try drying them out for reuse, it doesn't work. Past writers have recommended a bubble size of around 0.8mm (about $\frac{1}{30}$"). I find that in a skimmer as described above about the finest bubbles you can produce work well. Very fine ones would get swept back into the aquarium with the returning water but that doesn't happen.

Venturi skimmers use a fine tube with an intake from the air and a valve to

Many types and sizes of protein skimmers are available to hobbyists. Marine aquarists often prefer skimmers with very long columns set up alongside the tank, but more compact assemblies may work almost as well in some aquaria. Photo by V. Serbin.

prevent water outflow. Water passing this tube draws air into itself as fine bubbles. With a water column and collecting cup as before, water is pumped into the top of the tube with a swirling motion. The bubbles of air are carried down by a rapid flow of water and remain in contact for a long time. Eventually they rise into the collecting cup as the usual foam. External Venturis should be used with a reef tank, as with the counter current skimmers. In both cases some experimentation will be necessary to get the best results. It is also advisable to draw the water from the sump of the trickle filter, not the tank. This avoids sucking in unwanted material, even creatures! It also makes for less cluttering around the tank.

Recent practice has been to omit a trickle filter from the system, although a sump may still be retained. Dependence is on skimmers only, after the pre-filter. More than one may be used per aquarium. Although this may result in a setup with less reserve against fouling, it works. As far as I can ascertain, aquarists who have removed trickle filters

from the system have had a skimmer at work. This has, with little doubt, made the transition feasible. I feel that it would probably not be a successful move without a skimmer.

HEATING AND COOLING

It depends where you live whether you are likely to need heating, cooling or both. It also depends on whether you use metal halides. These, despite a fan, may heat the water excessively in a warm climate. Heaters are normally placed in the sump, two moderately powered heaters being safer

Every aquarium needs a thermometer, preferably the most accurate one you can afford. Simple strip thermometers work well for most applications. Photo courtesy Rolf C. Hagen Corp.

for a large tank than one powerful one. They will rarely both fail at once and if one sticks in the "on" position it stands less chance of overheating the aquarium. Set one heater a

of heat itself, oxygen depletion comes into the picture. At 21°C (70°F) sea water holds 5.2 ppm (parts per million) of oxygen. At 25°C (77°F) it holds 4.9 ppm and at 30°C (86°F) only 4.4

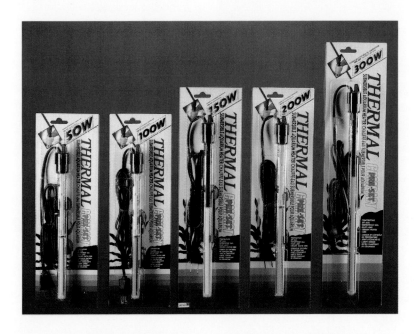

degree or two below the other. It will then turn on if the first one fails or is inadequate in cold weather.

Cooling systems are expensive but well worth while if your reef aquarium is likely to rise above 27°C (80°F). This can be hard on some soft corals. If a tank goes above about 30°C (86°F) many creatures may suffer. They suffer not only because

ppm. This is when saturated, which aquarium water rarely is. Anything less than 3 to 4 ppm affects sensitive organisms, so there isn't much margin.

A commercial cooling system draws water slowly from the sump and refrigerates it as it is returned. It has automatic controls. A number of types are usually available but if

switch the pump on and off. Seal off all entry and exit holes in the refrigerator to save power. You can then use it for normal purposes as well as for cooling the aquarium. A second-hand refrigerator will be much cheaper than a commercial cooling device.

That completes the requirements of a basic modern reef aquarium. There are many additional devices that you may choose to employ. There is also the question of automation of such devices. However, none of these added contrivances are really necessary. They may add to efficiency, saving of labor or safety, but extra equipment means extra cost. It also means more things that can go wrong.

ACTIVATED CARBON

Activated carbon or charcoal can be very useful for cleaning up the water. It removes many of the substances that are taken out by a protein skimmer. These include proteinaceous material, pigments and noxious gases, but not nitrogen cycle components. It is particularly helpful in producing sparkling clear water. A few ounces per 500

Submersible heaters, either with the thermostat separate from the heating element or combined in one unit, have been standard in aquaria for years. Photo courtesy Rolf C. Hagen Corp.

you don't have a local supply you can make one. Take a small domestic refrigerator and bore holes to pass a narrow gauge plastic tube in and out. Even an airline can suffice. Coil a few meters of tubing inside the refrigerator to cool the water effectively. With a very narrow tube the intake can be in a corner of the aquarium and the return made to the sump. It can be regulated with a simple valve. With a wider tube a water pump in the sump can be regulated to give a slow flow. If you don't mind a little wasted power, a heater can take care of overcooling. Otherwise, you may need a thermostat to liters (ca. 130 gals) of high grade carbon are enough. They will last for several months placed in a filter compartment or, less effectively, in a bag in the sump. Use a piece of fine stocking to contain the carbon.

Good activated carbon absorbs half its own weight of materials. Much of it around is unfortunately not that good. To be reasonably sure, use a gas-grade sample purchased from a specialist aquarium shop or from a chemical supply house. It is expensive, but worth it. The clumpy coals, shiny and quite large, are useless. A good brand is dull and finely divided into small granules.

POLYFILTERS, ETC.

Polymeric adsorbent pads take up all that carbon takes up and have a better affinity for heavy metals. They also take up some of the components of the nitrogen cycle. They may be used with or without carbon to do a more complete job. They last well, and gradually change color from dull white to almost black, when they should be discarded. Yet they are more rarely used than activated carbon and are unavailable in some countries.

Actually, with the heat produced from many types of lighting systems, heaters may not be necessary for the average reef aquarium. Many hobbyists find that they need cooling units instead. Photo by Dr. C. W. Emmens.

Ion-exchange resins of various types are a more controversial subject. They can be used to purify fresh water very effectively but their value in sea water is doubtful. Strongly active resins rapidly exchange their sodium ions for heavier metals -calcium, strontium, etc. They may thus remove desirable elements from the water as well as unwanted heavy metals. Mixtures of activated carbon and various resins are on the market. Some are recommended by the experts but on the whole are of unknown value.

DENITRATORS

These are special pieces of equipment designed to remove nitrates. They are complicated and not too easy to use. A slow flow of water from the aquarium passes through filters where anaerobic (reducing) bacteria convert nitrates back to nitrogen. The nitrogen then passes into the air. The process needs feeding with a source of energy such as lactose. Don't think of using one, it can cause trouble. A well-serviced reef tank does not produce nitrates.

If you have a problem with

The use of ion-exchange resins in the aquarium is new and not altogether certain at the moment. Many filter systems allow the hobbyist to experiment with resins and with adsorbent pads yet have the least potential for damaging results. Photo courtesy Ocean Clear Filters.

nitrates or phosphates, there are specific adsorbants for these substances. Use them for temporary removal of the trouble only. Then look for the reason it is happening and try to cure it.

CANISTER AND OTHER FILTERS

These filters, most of which are external to the aquarium, can be used instead of or as well as trickle filters. They can be adapted to do almost anything and may in fact replace all other filtration. Good ones are not cheap. They need more attention than trickle filters, and you cannot use them as a sump for other purposes, but some aquarists like to add them to do a super job.

REDOX POTENTIAL METERS

Equipment to measure the oxidation-reduction potential of aquarium water is becoming popular. This is a complex chemical concept that expresses in the end the power of the water to reduce or oxidize substances. We want a good—but not too powerful—oxidizing potential. It is measured in millivolts, always a positive quantity for oxidation. A denitrator would have a negative redox potential.

Canister filters are available in both internal (the filter is placed inside the tank) and external models. The Fluval 2 model by Rolf C. Hagen Corp. is one of the internal models.

Redox potential is usually measured with a platinum electrode and a reference electrode of silver chloride. Natural sea water potentials run at around 400 millivolts. In satisfactory aquaria a potential of between 200 and 400 millivolts is found although the lower level is to be avoided. It promotes blue-green algal growth. But a reliable measurement is difficult to make, requiring careful preparation of the electrodes. The platinum one must be in position for some time to give an accurate recording. The equipment is expensive and used mostly in Germany, where it is regarded as necessary by some serious aquarists. You probably won't need it unless you are a devoted gadgeteer.

OZONE

Triatomic oxygen, O_3, readily breaks down to O_2, normal oxygen, giving off an oxygen atom that combines with anything it can. It kills off bacteria and protozoa and readily damages higher organisms. Generated by special equipment, it should only be used in a protein skimmer followed by a carbon filter. This prevents a damaging amount from entering the tank. As it oxidizes vitamins as well as pollutants, ozone should be used with caution. It raises the redox potential also, sometimes to dangerous levels.

ULTRAVIOLET LIGHT (U/V)

This is a safer method than using ozone as long as it is shielded from damaging your eyes and skin, macroalgae, invertebrates and vertebrates. It is particularly dangerous to look at a U/V tube. Glass or plastic acts as an adequate shield. Active at 2,000 to 3,000 angstroms, it is generated by special fluorescent tubes. Water in a thin shell passes over the tubes, killing microorganisms. U/V is used in sterilizing water, in quarantine setups and as a cure for diseases. It is not used by most aquarists and is rarely necessary in a reef tank that remains healthy on its own if properly run.

AUTOMATION

You can spend many thousands of dollars installing automatic controls. There are gadgets

Only in the cleanest water will mushroom anemones, *Actinodiscus*, display their brightest colors. Photo by M. & C. Piednoir.

Ozonizers are popular with advanced hobbyists; they are used to help kill bacteria and protozoans in the aquarium. Ozonizers should be used only by those familiar with the effects of ozone. Photo courtesy Ultralife Reef Products.

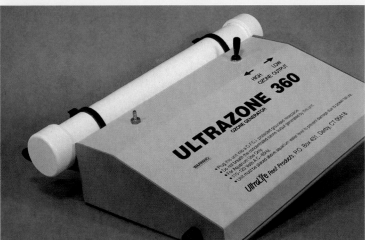

to stabilize automatically pH, redox potential, water levels etc. There are reactors to help control nitrates, oxygen, carbonate hardness and ozone. The only ones I use are automatic light switches. If you are away from home frequently some degree of automation can be very helpful. Otherwise, you may spend as long looking after the gadgets as doing the job yourself. They have to be checked, parts renewed or cleaned and so forth. Also, it is necessary to plan ahead for the installation of whatever you feel you might eventually install. Insufficient room under or around the tank, not enough holes drilled, inadequate power supplies or outlets are all possibilities. I have seen set-ups where it seems difficult to determine which is the reef tank at first glance, particularly from the rear. Never forget that a "window on the sea" effect is the real aim of a reef aquarium. Something looking like an engine room is not what we want.

Always remember that the function of the reef aquarium is to provide a "window to the sea" effect, not test the limits of your technology and wallet. Photo by Dr. C. W. Emmens.

CHAPTER 3
Starting Up

In addition to the equipment listed in the first chapter, we need more to treat the tap or other water that will be used. Most of us have to depend on synthetic salts with which to make up our salt water. Even if you live near the sea, the available marine water may be too foul to use. Once in the aquarium the water needs constant checking. For this, many kits are offered. We shall need to make an informed choice of these.

MAKE-UP WATER

The water to be used for making up synthetic salt water must be reasonably pure. **Most tap water is not!** Although at least theoretically fit for human consumption it often contains nitrates, chlorine or chloramines, heavy metals and other undesirables. An obvious alternative is distilled water (glass distilled not copper distilled!). This is likely to be far too expensive. A more realistic possibility is water from a soft drink factory.

Otherwise, tap water must be purified as far as feasible. The best procedure is to use either demineralized water or reverse osmosis water. For the former, ion exchange resins are used, perhaps with activated carbon.

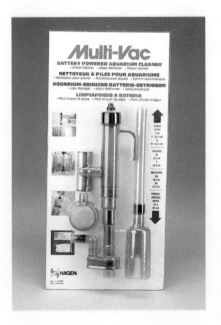

Keeping the aquarium clean is a continuing problem, but many manufacturers market tank vacuums that work well. Photo courtesy Rolf C. Hagen Corp.

Commercial water purifiers may do all that is necessary, but check to make sure of any particular brand. It pays to get an analysis of your local water from the suppliers, then you know what to expect. Reverse osmosis equipment is expensive but produces pure water. It depends on forcing water molecules through a semi-permeable membrane that keeps everything else behind.

If you are lucky and your tap water isn't too bad, you can use a simple technique. I pass tap water slowly through a cylinder of activated carbon. It trickles

designed to eliminate chloramines and to bind heavy metals. The water is then safe for immediate use. I do not guarantee that this works everywhere. Water purified by resins or reverse osmosis is a safer bet.

Sea water itself can be treated by my method. If it has particulate matter in it, pass it through a sand filter first, then the carbon. I am

Starter kits provide the beginner with the basic equipment necessary to set up a tank. Many kits are available to fit any budget. Photo courtesy Rolf C. Hagen Corp.

through 20cm (8") in a 8cm (3") diameter vessel at about 4 liters (1 gal) per 5 minutes. You could run it quicker through a longer cylinder. I then add 1 ml per 4 liters (1 in 4000) of Sera's Aqutan, one of the compounds

lucky to be able to get sea water that has already been filtered from a local aquarium. I then add Aqutan as above and again find it safe for use. It is sparkling clear - it has to be for viewing specimens through meters of water in an oceanarium. It is inshore, harbor water and so I avoid receiving it in bad weather. However, the aquarium has to use it then and its fishes and invertebrates survive, even without Aqutan. But it doesn't remain in the system as in a home aquarium, being soon flushed away by new, purer, water.

Although you have a water pet-shop copper kit should not detect any for safety. The same water will be used for replacing evaporation and so should be occasionally tested. If you are using an efficient demineralizing setup or reverse osmosis this is hardly necessary. Make sure in the former case that the resins remain active. A replacement or reactivation

Your pet shop will be able to provide you with all the necessary equipment—and gadgets—you want for your reef aquarium. Photo courtesy Rolf C. Hagen Corp.

board analysis of their water your own pipes may add copper to it. If this is possible, test it for copper before and after treating the make-up water to be sure that no significant level of the free metal remains. Your schedule will be issued with the equipment. Activated carbon cannot be reactivated, whatever other sources may tell you. At least, not at home. It needs a very high temperature.

The varied invertebrates and plants in this aquarium did not spring up overnight. The reef aquarium needs time to develop to its full beauty. Photo by Dr. C. W. Emmens.

SYNTHETIC SALTS

There are a number of good brands of salts available. Prefer one that gives an analysis of its contents, also, one that can be measured out from the package when you don't need all of it. Some brands do not mix the ingredients thoroughly - consult your dealer. If you compare the amounts of the various constituents in the package with natural sea water you will find differences. For some reason, most are short on calcium. There is usually an excess of iron and of trace elements. This is because these are rapidly lost, so don't worry. Calcium can be made up as dealt with below; it is regularly lost to growing corals, etc. anyway.

When first filling the aquarium, dump the required amount of salts in and then add the water. Nothing else should be in the tank at that stage. The salts may come as a one-shot package or with trace elements to be added later. Fill the tank right up to get the water circulating via the pre-filter. Later, you will have to remove some of the water as other things are added.

When making periodic water changes, it is best to aerate the new mix for a day or so in a suitable container. It will then be less of a shock to the inhabitants of the aquarium since newly mixed salts can be quite toxic. With natural sea water, this doesn't matter. It should be used either immediately or only after several weeks storage. This is because bacteria proliferate during the first days of storage and later precipitate out. So does any plankton or particulate matter. Storage in the dark is best to prevent algal growth.

TEST KITS

Kits purchased from a pet shop are adequate for all normal purposes, although they do not measure very small quantities of the substances in question. Instead they usually cover the range below which you need not worry about and above which is dangerous. They also vary in accuracy. It is best to choose one in which a sample of aquarium water is tested against a series of liquid controls. Testing against a color chart is less accurate except where a sudden change in color is expected, as in a calcium or carbonate hardness test.

SPECIFIC GRAVITY

This (and a thermometer, I suppose) is the only test requiring a special instrument, either a hydrometer or a test vessel. Make sure at which temperature your instrument measures. Standard ones express the specific gravity (S.G.) as at

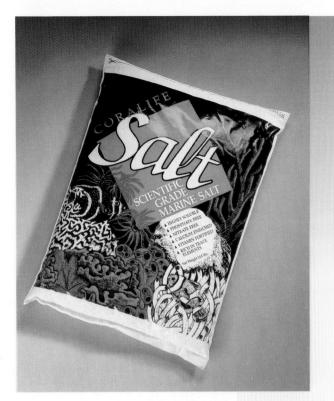

Almost all aquarists today use synthetic salt mixes in their aquaria because of consistent quality lacking in natural sea water. Photo courtesy Coralife.

15°C (59°F) and when used in warm water they give a lower reading. But there are some specially made for a 24°C (75°F) reading that give a figure as if the water were at 15°C.

With a standard hydrometer meant for 15°C a normal sea water specific gravity of 1.025 will be read as 1.022 at 24°C. With one meant for 24°C it will read 1.025. Reports in the literature usually leave one undecided as to which is meant. We usually take a S.G. of 1.022 to mean diluted sea water or its equivalent.

pH

The pH or hydrogen ion concentration on a log scale of normal sea water is 8.2 to 8.3. We aim for this in the aquarium but it usually tends to fall. Don't let it fall below 8.0 in a reef tank. It <u>can</u> rise above 8.3, but rarely does. Don't worry unless it exceeds 8.5. Then turn off the lights and it will gradually fall. The pH can be increased by adding sodium bicarbonate ($NaHCO_3$). It will rise gradually over the next two days. Do not use sodium carbonate (Na_2CO_3) or sodium hydroxide (caustic soda, $NaOH$). They both give sudden rises and then a fall. Pellets supplied with pH kits are made of one of these or a mixture of them. Discard them. One level teaspoon per 80 liters (ca 20 gals) of $NaHCO_3$ increases the pH by 0.1 approx.

COPPER

This kit is for use only with make-up water, as you should never introduce copper into the aquarium. Copper kits are not particularly accurate. It doesn't matter since you aim at finding none at all in any water going into the aquarium. Sea water should never show any measurable copper by a hobbyist's kit although there is a minute amount present. Some flake fish foods contain too much copper. Ask the manufacturer if the food you like contains copper.

NITROGEN COMPOUNDS

The products of the nitrogen cycle, ammonia, nitrites and nitrates, may all be measured. Results should be expressed as ammonia-nitrogen, nitrite-nitrogen and nitrate-nitrogen. If they are given as the full compound you can use correction factors to convert to nitrogen equivalents. This is important since the nitrogen content is usually quoted in the literature. The correction factors are: for ammonia x 0.82, for nitrites x 0.30 and for nitrates x 0.23.

Modern ammonia kits are quite accurate. They previously were not! You can measure the rise and fall of ammonia at the beginning of the conditioning of a newly set-up tank, followed by that of nitrites and later nitrates. This is described in almost any text on the subject. Later, all should be very low in a reef tank. Desirable amounts are ammonia zero, nitrites less than 0.1 ppm and nitrates less than 5 ppm.

PHOSPHATES

Phosphates promote microalgae and hair algae and are best kept well below 1 ppm. They are fairly toxic to some invertebrates as well and inhibit coral growth. The usual tests measure inorganic phosphates. Organic phosphates bound to proteins, etc. are removed by protein skimmers and so should remain low.

CARBONATE HARDNESS

Closely related to pH, carbonate hardness or alkalinity is an important factor in the reef tank. Corals, other invertebrates and calcareous algae remove calcium carbonate from the water continuously in daylight. Both calcium and carbonate ions thus need constant replacement. Commercial buffers are available to increase both, together with other components. Alternatively you can decide to add calcium and carbonates separately yourself. A simple, safe way to do this is with sodium bicarbonate as recommended for pH enhancement. Calcium is added as detailed next.

Carbonate hardness is most frequently expressed in German degrees of hardness (dKH). Several other systems exist, the most important of which are the English Clark unit and ppm of $CaCO_3$. One dKH is 18 ppm, one Clark unit is 14 ppm of $CaCO_3$ approx. Sea water is rather weakly buffered at 6 or 7 dKH, and many aquarists choose to keep their tanks at a higher value. This gives greater pH stability, particularly if much carbon dioxide is generated. Carbon dioxide is purposely added to promote algal growth by some and then a really high dKH may be needed - up to 18. Coral growth is indirectly assisted via the zooxanthellae. I like a dKH of about 9, a little above normal, and my own corals grow too much for my liking already.

CALCIUM

An easy way of keeping up the calcium level in the aquarium is to add it to the water used to make up for evaporation. With the usual open top, evaporation is considerable. A drip or levelling system must be used over the sump. If you dump too much lime water (kalkwasser) in at once the pH shoots up. Lime water is a solution of calcium hydroxide (slaked lime; $Ca(OH)_2$). It can be made up by shaking quicklime, CaO, *carefully* in water. *Carefully*, because the solution gets hot. Not much CaO will dissolve; leave the rest to settle out. $Ca(OH)_2$ itself takes too long to dissolve.

By this method, you must monitor the calcium content of the water frequently. It may rise too high or even not enough. Sea water has 410 ppm, near to saturation. Keep the aquarium at around 450 ppm but no higher. Kits usually measure in jumps of up to 50 ppm so you can't be very accurate. They depend on a change in indicator color.

Calcium chloride ($CaCl_2$) is much more soluble than CaO and may be added as a concentrated solution. It does not raise the pH or the carbonate hardness, except to supply the needed calcium for the latter. It can therefore be used weekly or as often as you like. The effect on calcium concentration must be checked as above. The absorption of calcium by corals, other invertebrates and calcareous algae is considerable. An unsupplemented tank can lose 20 or 30 ppm per week. Corals in particular can suffer and hair algae seem to be encouraged when a significant fall occurs. It is therefore most important to keep the calcium concentration high.

OXYGEN

Measuring the oxygen content of water used to be a complicated procedure. New one-shot tests are now available to make an easy task of it. I don't know just how accurate they are, but you can judge from the following. When all is well a reef aquarium should have saturated or near-saturated oxygen levels. They can even be super saturated in bright light with much algae. Then oxygen bubbles will be seen rising from the algae. So a test in such conditions should show saturation.

Different regions of an aquarium will show different oxygen levels. With a good circulation and a trickle filter the open water should read around 5.0 ppm at a typical temperature of 23°-25°C (73°-77°F).

the animals tells you all you need to know. But they are also very meticulous about caring for their aquaria and mostly use natural sea water and give frequent large changes. With natural sea water you do not get the shocking effect of salts. The ones who do little testing

Does this tank have the proper carbonate hardness? Is the nitrate level too high? Has evaporation caused the specific gravity to rise beyond acceptable levels? Only the proper test kit can answer these and many other questions before the plants and animals in the tank suffer. Photo by Dr. C. W. Emmens.

WHICH KITS TO USE?

To know what is happening in your aquarium, all of the above kits are needed. Yet I know some successful reef keepers who only test pH and specific gravity, perhaps occasionally nitrates. They work on the theory that observing the condition of

and are careless of maintenance are those who get into strife.

I test regularly for pH, specific gravity, nitrates, phosphates, calcium and carbonate hardness, every few weeks. I would only rush out and get an ammonia, nitrite or oxygen kit if symptoms suggested it. They never have. I use natural sea water, but only change 5% per week. I make up calcium regularly, knowing from past experience how much to add of a commercial $Ca(OH)_2$ + $CaCl_2$ solution. I also add 5 ml per 400 liters (100 gallons) per week of a 10% solution of strontium chloride. This aids in the utilization of calcium and helps greatly in the keeping of difficult corals like *Acropora*. I do not use any automation except for the lighting. I do not use ozone, U/V, CO_2 additions, denitrification, redox potential measurements or anything of that ilk. *High-tech vendors hate me!* I should really install cooling because just occasionally my tanks get too hot, up to 29°C (84°F) or so. But I have only lost two soft corals from that cause and so go on risking it. If a tank looks like overheating I turn off the lights, just for a day or so at most. With metal halides, this keeps the tank cooler and the fishes less active.

LIVING ROCK

This is simply dead coral, usually impacted somewhat, on which all kinds of organisms have grown. A

Living rock provides the basis of all reef aquarium setups, serving as the provider of the resting stages of many invertebrates that will appear in the tank within weeks of introduction of the rocks. Photo by Bill Chung.

Correctly regenerating living rock requires delicate filtration for one or two weeks until the invertebrates and plants recover. Undergravel filters with powerheads are adequate for this function. Photo courtesy Rolf C. Hagen Corp.

very great deal depends on the quality of the rock you obtain. If you can, get shipments of newly gathered rock straight from the supplier. Unless he can vary the place from which he gets it, obtain some from different suppliers if possible. The purpose of all this is to get as great a variety of life as possible. So don't proceed to destroy most of it by treating the living rock as some advise. Put it into a tank with a filter after cleaning off any dead or decaying stuff, perhaps also any large sponges, but no more. Shake out and search out small crabs and mantis shrimps. These can grow up to be terrible nuisances. Circulate the water briskly for a week or two with frequent partial charges until no smell, clouding or dying off occurs. Use a low light level, say around 10,000 lux. You will need three or four batches treated at intervals. By this technique most of the algae and animals will survive, so you will start off with a good variety of life in good condition. If your pet shop does all this for you so much the better. The filter can be

trickle, canister or undergravel just so long as it does a good, brief job.

Good living rock is shipped anywhere in some countries. You can even specify its rough

composition - algae, tube worms, sea squirts and so on. If you cannot get it, you may have to accept material shipped dry. This is half dead and has lost much of its original content but will recover to a surprising extent. Treat it just as above. It may take a long time to regrow algae, perhaps tunicates and some soft coral and sponges. Tube worms and small critters hidden in crevices will also survive. Try to get at least a few pieces of good living rock that will help the dried stuff to repopulate.

By keeping illumination low (i.e. a few hours per day if you cannot gradually increase intensity), sponges and other organisms that live in poorly illuminated places will survive. Other light-loving creatures will survive until given fuller lighting. Since we want the sponges, sea squirts, etc. to keep going, place the first batch when ready along the back and base of the aquarium. This will eventually be covered by other rock. Do not pack it tightly but leave plenty of room for free circulation. Place spiky pieces spikes downward so as to jack up the reef. Some aquarists use egg crate or whatever for the same purpose - good circulation.

This first batch of rock is now used to condition the aquarium. Forget all you've been told about other conditioning methods. Set everything going and after a week start to measure the nitrite level. You can do ammonia first if you like, but it isn't necessary. A

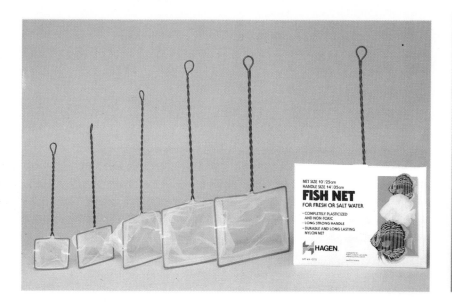

Don't forget to purchase at least a couple of sizes and shapes of aquarium nets. You'll find that nets are much more important than you might think and you never have enough when you need one **now**. Photo courtesy Rolf C. Hagen Corp.

nitrite peak will occur soon and fall off. Then you can add the next batch of rock, so start it up early on. As the reef grows, gradually increase illumination.

The next batch of rock is built upon the first. Leave spaces as before plus ledges on which further introductions will be placed. After one or more further treated batches, you will end up with a sloping reef running from near to the top at the rear to near to the base at the front. If you run into difficulties in fitting it all together, use tooth picks or even chewing gum (well chewed!) and drill holes for linkage if necessary. A further nitrite peak may happen with batch number two as a first peak does not necessarily mean a fully conditioned aquarium.

In the past, much stress has been laid on chemical conditioning with ammonium salts. They are supposed to encourage the growth of *Nitrosomonas* bacteria, later of *Nitrobacter* to complete the nitrogen cycle. So they may, but it is a mistake to suppose that this condition, displacing heterotrophic bacteria, will persist. Instead, the

proportions of various bacteria depend on demand. If the ammonia being produced naturally increases, so will *Nitrosomonas*. If it falls, so will *Nitrosomonas* concentration. And so on. Other bacteria have to be there to produce the ammonia once you stop adding it.

A difficulty with chemical conditioning is that an excess of nitrates is produced, a nuisance to be dealt with from the start. I know, I have recommended it in earlier writing. Well, I was wrong. It does enable you to add corals and fishes, etc. soon after building the reef. And you can put in all of the reef at once. But it is otherwise no advantage in the long run and costly to operate. You can still use it for fish-only tanks, but not for reef aquaria.

ADDING FURTHER CREATURES

Once the reef is built and everything is in order, more can be added. Not all at once, but just a few specimens per week, depending on sizes for how many. It is best to keep to

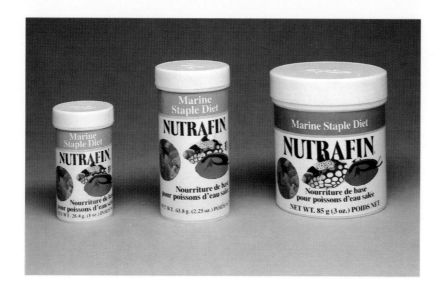

fairly small corals and only partially-grown other invertebrates. They will grow up and start overcrowding soon enough, so be cautious. Keep tabs on how things are going, measure the pH once a week at first. The same with specific gravity, calcium concentration and nitrites. Occasionally, check nitrates, phosphates and calcium hardness. Start using a protein skimmer early on. Also add strontium if you want good coral growth. Molybdenum is added in addition by some aquarists. It is needed by all algae and seems to be, like strontium, an element they tend to run short of easily.

Fishes can be introduced quite early, the most docile ones first. When you add others, they are less likely to be attacked by them as they were first claimants to the site. Being the most docile, they will also tend to leave others alone. The most useful first fishes are the hair algae eaters. Avoid any that may eat macroalgae or corals or attack invertebrates. If you intend keeping a variety of shrimps, omit the popular *Stenopus hispidus*, the banded coral shrimp. They grow large and belligerent and will often kill other species.

All kinds of algae are likely to grow from the living rock. Most of them need a

rock for attachment and cannot be introduced as pieces very successfully. The genus *Caulerpa* is an exception. There are many different, attractive species that have made them very popular. They can be grown from fragments that will soon attach themselves to substrates. Their main disadvantage is dying off suddenly. They turn white within a day or two and will pollute the water if not immediately removed. A warning of this being about to happen is the presence of tiny hairs on the fronds, a reproductive phenomenon. Otherwise *Caulerpa* is a rapid grower and helps to absorb nitrates from the water as it grows. Cropped regularly, it can be a significant denitrator.

Other algae grow relatively slowly and are preferred by some because they need less attention. Green algae like *Caulerpa* may be soft and attract many fishes, but the calcareous (limey) ones are not so edible. So *Halimeda* and *Udotea* species are favored, with their hard, cactus-like plates or fans. Many of the red algae, which can stand dimmer light, are also calcareous and popular in the aquarium. Brown algae that grow from living rock are usually welcome, but beware of introducing others. They often die off, turning mushy and toxic in the process. Algae have various alternations of generations and the progeny of a species in your tank may look quite different from their parent generation.

CHAPTER 4
Porifera and Cnidaria

In this and the following chapter I shall give space to each phylum appropriate to its importance to the reef aquarium. So some well-known creatures like the octopus will hardly get a mention. There are around two dozen animal phyla and the aquarist may care to ponder over the fact that his favorite fishes are all in one class in the phylum Chordata. The invertebrates cover a terrific variety of body plans, habits and requirements compared with them. It is a tribute to those who have helped to develop the modern reef tank that so many of them can be kept together.

PORIFERA

The sponges are a very ancient group and the simplest multicellular animals. They go back in fossil form to 650 million years ago. They are not easy to keep in the aquarium. They mostly want poor lighting and plenty of filter foods, difficult to supply without fouling the tank. The sponge is in fact a very efficient filter that deals with many gallons of water in a short space of time. It is estimated that one the size of a fist pumps over 4,000 liters (1,000 gallons) per day.

What usually happens in the aquarium is that any sponges on the live rock gradually disappear. Some may even die quickly and need removal. Perhaps the odd one will survive in a dim corner or at the back. New ones may sometimes appear in similar places and thrive, but it is a chancy business. The result is that they are usually cleaned off new living rock as a precaution. If any reappear, good luck to them. It is not worth trying to feed them unless you can supply tiny live marine plankton. Newly hatched brine shrimp are often too big for small sponges to filter off.

CNIDARIA (COELENTERATA)

The corals, anemones,

As pollution and environmental laws place more and more restrictions on the availability of coral skeletons for use in the aquarium, artificial corals have become more available in pet shops. Some lines look as good or better than the real thing, last longer, and pose no environmental problems. Photo courtesy Tetra/Second Nature.

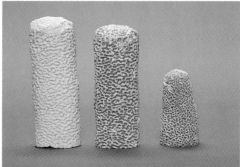

Feeding invertebrates no longer has to be complicated and time-consuming. Prepared invertebrate foods now are widely available and reliable. They should be used frugally to avoid fouling the aquarium. Photo courtesy Coralife.

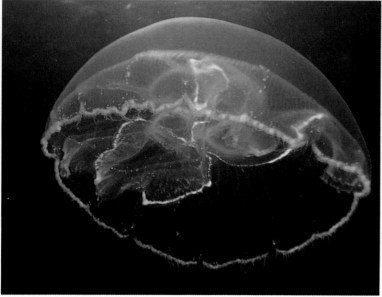

Jellyfishes, with very few exceptions, cannot be kept for long periods in the average home aquarium. Most species, such as this moon jelly, *Aurelia aurita*, live only short adult lives even in the ocean. Photo by C. Platt.

etc., are also primitive, but in great contrast to the sponges. They have musculature, a gut, sense organs and something of a nervous system. They have also developed stinging cells characteristic of the phylum, the cnidoblasts or nematoblasts. The alternative name of Coelenterata refers to the fact that the gut is also the body cavity. Each individual is a double-walled sac, with a mouth but no anus. The outer wall is the ectoderm and the inner the endoderm. Between them is the mesoglea, collagen fibers making up a sort of connective tissue that is not cellular.

The animal comes in two forms with the same basic structure, although they look very different. The first is a polyp, which may be solitary as in the anemone or colonial as in most corals. The second is a medusa (jellyfish) that floats freely in the water and may alternate with the polyp stage. Polyps bud off medusae that give rise to germ cells that unite to form more polyps. In other species, there are only polyps.

In the aquarium we are primarily interested in the polyps. The appearance of medusae will be interesting but they are going to have a hard time of it. Some will be eaten, some get filtered off. It will be a miracle if any succeed in reproducing. The polyp has a base attached to a substrate of some kind, a mouth at the other end with a ring or rings of tentacles. The tentacles carry nematoblasts that may also occur elsewhere. Each nematoblast cell has a long, hollow inverted filament that is forced out of the cell on contact. It may just spear the object it touches, or inject a poison as well.

HYDROZOA

There are three classes of Cnidaria, of which the hydrozoans are probably the most primitive. They alternate generations of polyps and medusae in most species but some have only polyps. The medusae are usually quite small, of the type sometimes seen in the aquarium - pulsating little saucers that feed on plankton. Soft-bodied hydrozoans form mats on rocks and shells, such as *Hydractina. Clava* and *Tubularia* cover seaweeds and have no medusae. In contrast *Physalia*, the Portuguese man of war, is a larger colonial floating species with a float, specialized polyps for feeding and attached medusa-like gonophores for reproduction. There are many others, but few do well in the aquarium. They need plankton or a substitute and do not have zooxanthellae like corals. Nor do the hydrocorals, looking like true corals, such as the famous fire coral, *Millepora*.

SCYPHOZOA

These are the jellyfishes. Usually large and dangerous in an aquarium, some have polyp stages but others do not. They are of separate sexes and so sperm from a male must find its way into a female. She then frees large numbers of larvae that either develop into more medusae or into polyps that bud off medusae.

ANTHOZOA

Now we come to the class of real interest to aquarists - the corals and anemones. They are divided into several subclasses all of importance to reef keepers. There are only polyps, no medusae.

OCTOCORALLIA

This subclass is characterized by possessing eight tentacles per polyp. The order Alcyonacea, or soft corals, may or may not have indwelling algae, the zooxanthellae. Those that do are obviously easiest to keep in the aquarium as they can survive without solid food. Others may have to be fed specially, but some seem to get along even without plankton or "invertebrate" food. They must find the particulate matter floating around or dissolved organics sufficient. Most alcyonaceans have spicules in a fleshy body carrying many polyps, which may differ spectacularly in color from the trunk from which they emerge. In an unusual species, *Tubipora musica*, the spicules coalesce to form a rigid red skeleton carrying brown or green polyps.

The family Alcyonidae has a group of very successful octocorals in the aquarium. They have zooxanthellae and live normally in shallow, brightly lit conditions. No special feeding is needed, the bright light in a reef tank is enough to keep them nourished via their algae. Some are so tough that they

Cnidarians form the basis for most reef aquaria today. Here the coral *Euphyllia* and a small sea pen grasp center stage. With luck and attention these colonies will prosper and may even reproduce. Photo by Dr. C. W. Emmens.

can be cut down to size when they grow too large. *Sarcophyton* is a genus of large mushroom-like octocorals that look rather horrible until decorative polyps emerge. *Xenia* has fringed polyps, white, brown, blue or green in color. *Anthelia* has fat stalks of just brown or whitish polyps that are attractive because they pulsate continuously to catch prey. There are many others, from tiny encrusting forms to tree-like species.

The Nephtheidae have no zooxanthellae but some very attractive members. Both the flesh and the spicules may be colored, often differently. Regrettably, they need special conditions to flourish. Given dim lighting and special feeding they will grow and reproduce. This may be possible in a shaded area of a reef tank, but the frequent feeding needed is a problem. It tends to foul the tank as most of it is inevitably wasted. However, nitrate and phosphate removers and plenty of skimming may make it possible. *Dendronephthya* has pride of place. It may come with white polyps on a red or yellow body, with or without differently colored spicules or there may be red polyps or yellow polyps on a white, red or yellow body and so on. *Eunephthya* and *Lithophyton* are almost equally attractive.

The Gorgonacea, or sea fans, are similar in requirements and need strong currents in addition. They are very colorful and look splendid when first put into the aquarium. Unless conditions are right they will degenerate or become blocked by hair algae. Most species form a flat tangle of horny branches covered by a fleshy outer coating. Polyps are embedded in the coating and feed on microplankton brought to them by the current of water they face. Algae-eating fishes or snails are the best hope of keeping them clean if necessary. The many genera are hard to identify and there seems little point in naming some of them. The same species may be found in many colors and color combinations as with the Nephtheidae.

The Pennatulacea, or sea pens, come from sandy bottoms and are not suitable for reef tanks. They need a deep substrate.

ZOANTHARIA

A subclass of greatest interest to the aquarist, the zoantharians come in six orders. These include the hard corals, anemones, tube anemones, zoanthids and leather corals.

ACTINIARIA

This order comprises the sea anemones. They are solitary, never form a skeleton but may occur in dense colonies of separate individuals - each an independent polyp. Anemones can close up to form a jelly-like blob when disturbed. Their drawback in a crowded tank is a liability to wander around, coming into conflict with other creatures. Good lighting with a fairly brisk current may convince a specimen to stay put. Some have zooxanthellae but many do not. Species from cooler waters will not stand tropical conditions and should not be purchased.

The Nynantheae, a suborder, contains many popular tropical species as well as temperate ones. The giant anemones, the Stichodactylines, with which anemone fishes associate, are familiar to most aquarists. They carry zooxanthellae which enable them to survive and grow without further feeding. *Stichodactyla* species look like terry towelling, with short clubbed tentacles, while *Heteractis* has longer tentacles and is less of a stinger. The many species are rarely correctly identified. The commonest color is purplish-brown but red, orange or, very rarely, blue individuals occur. Some are sometimes found bright green.

Tealia is another large anemone but not as big as the giants. It grows to about 30cm (1 ft) in diameter. With a red body and medium long tentacles that may be red, yellow, green or mixed in color, it is very attractive. Anemone fishes also like it.

Some species of *Anemonia* occur in the Mediterranean Sea and will stand tropical conditions but prefer it a little cooler. They have zooxanthellae and so need bright light. *A. sulcata* has about 200 tentacles and cannot close right up - so it has super stinging powers in compensation. Beware!

SCLERACTINIA

This is the order of stony

The common anemones seen with their clownfishes often are species of *Heteractis*, formerly known as *Radianthus*. The long, often swaying, tentacles distinguish this genus from *Stichodactyla*, the other common clownfish anemones. Photo by Dr. C. W. Emmens.

corals, reef builders, although some do not build reefs and live as solitary polyps. In contrast to the anemones, very few species can stand cool water and flourish only at around 24°-27°C (75°-80°F), even a little higher. Water must be of top quality and well oxygenated. The indwelling alga is usually *Gymnodinium microadriaticum*, yellow-brown in color. It assists in the laying down of calcium and provides sufficient nourishment to maintain most corals. A high calcium level in the water, around 450 ppm, and maintenance of strontium levels help. The corals have developed a clever trick to utilize the algal products. They produce enzymes that cause the algae to leak most of their manufactured sugars, amino acids and fats.

Since the stony corals are normally classified by the structure of their skeletons it is often very difficult to identify them. They vary in color within a single species and can look very different when growing in different conditions. However, we get to know those commonly available just by appearance and have to guess the probable identity of others. Most corals open by night to catch the plankton that then abounds. Perhaps 10% open by day, some by day and night. These are the ones of most interest, although some of the others look nice even when retracted. Polyps can vary in size from almost microscopic to 60cm (2 ft) in diameter.

FAVIIDAE

The largest family of corals, containing the brain corals, has some species that open by day - day corals for short. Examples are *Favia speciosa* and *Favites* sp. They can be brown or green and do well in the aquarium. The genus *Goniastrea*, brain corals, has many members that look colored and interesting despite opening only at night.

CARYOPHYLLIIDAE

Popular hermatypic (reef-building and algae carrying) corals in this family are the *Euphyllia* species. *E. glabrescens* has blue to green tentacles with white or green tips. *E. ancora* has blue to orange tentacles with hammer-shaped tips. *E. divisa* has many fine brown or green tentacles with white round knobs as tips. All are day corals, very attractive and easy to keep - in the right conditions.

The genus *Catalaphyllia*, elegant or elegance corals, has only two species. *C. jardinei* has bright green stripes on a large oval disc and green or brown tentacles with pink or white tips. *C. plicata* is almost an albino version of it, with pale tentacles and disc. Polyps of both are large, up to 12cm (5") across. These corals do well in a reef tank, but show their disapproval of poor conditions by peeling off the skeleton.

The bubble corals are in this family, *Plerogyra* and *Physogyra*. They have grape-like vesicles by day and normal tentacles at night. Both are attractive phases. The vesicles are supposed to protect the tentacles during the day, but as they are withdrawn it seems unlikely to me. These corals need feeding at night as they are without zooxanthellae. They can take chunks of fish or shrimp as the polyps are large and voracious.

PORITIDAE
The genus *Porites* has many species with tiny polyps, some opening by day. They are favorite homes for tube worms that help to decorate them. Most are brown, but odd colonies are found that are brightly colored. The genus *Goniopora* is very popular, both with aquarists and dealers. Why? Because they are tough, aggressive day corals that look very attractive but usually die after about six months. So the aquarist buys another one. I don't know why almost everyone reports failure with *Goniopora* because mine live for years and bud off young colonies. *Goniopora* has 24 tentacles, usually brown, whereas *Alveopora* has 12. Otherwise, they are very similar. *A. marionensis* and *A. fenestrata* do well in the reef tank, many others do not. They are brown or greenish with a rare pink variety in each case, not often offered. The genus as a whole is uncommon and found in isolated places where they may be abundant over a small area.

ACROPORIDAE
A very large family with many genera of corals with

Colonies of *Goniopora*, such as the one at the top of this aquarium, are hardy and open during the day, but in the hands of many aquarists they only live a few months. Photo by Dr. C. W. Emmens.

tiny polyps. Some are encrusting forms that open by day but even those that do not are often pretty and vividly colored, red, pink and blue. The genera *Anacropora, Montipora* and *Astreopora* seem promising but little used. The staghorns, genus *Acropora*, were very difficult to keep until the discovery that high calcium levels plus strontium are needed. Now many are having success with them.

POCILLOPORIDAE

Much of the same remarks as for the Acroporidae apply here. Many are branching corals and few, if any, open in daylight. Nevertheless, there are attractive, highly colored species well worth keeping. *Pocillopora verrucosa* is a common example, found in brown, green, pink or blue colonies.

FUNGIIDAE

Most members of this family are solitary, including the mushroom corals. These have large single polyps that are not reef-building. *Heliofungia actiniformis* opens by day, with long green, purple or pale white-tipped tentacles. *Fungia* has shorter tentacles and stays closed by day. Most species do well in the reef tank if well lit with metal halides and may open in moderate light in contrast to their natural habit. *Polyphyllia* is an oblong genus that opens by day and has green or brown tentacles. It looks like a *Euphyllia*.

MUSSIDAE

A family notorious for dying in the aquarium is yielding better success with modern treatment. *Cynarina* is a genus of solitary, large corals that does well and is open by night but has semi-transparent vesicles by day, greenish or brown. *Lobophyllia* and *Isophyllastrea* also have an attractive appearance by day and are not solitary.

PECTINIIDAE

Related to the Mussidae, the Pectiniidae are often full of color. The genus *Pectinia* apparently includes some of the most beautiful corals in the world, tree-like and very colorful. Yet they do not seem to be kept, perhaps because they fail in the aquarium or have done so in the past. They should be tried with calcium and strontium supplementation. *Echinophyllia* and *Oxypora* are other genera that form colored plates or encrustations, should be very easy to keep, but rarely appear for sale.

DENDROPHYLLIIDAE

Although found on reefs, these algae-less corals are not reef builders and live in sheltered places. They are popular because of their striking colors. However, they do not usually do too well in the aquarium. They need fine or planktonic food and just don't seem to get enough to flourish. The genus *Dendrophyllia* has yellow or orange polyps, opening at night but still attractive by day. *Tubastraea* is similar but gets very large in nature. So is *Balanophyllia*, which opens by day. *Duncanopsammia* from deep waters opens by day and night and looks good in the blue-grey variety. If you try to keep them - they are worth a try - put them in a shaded area where you can get at them easily to feed them.

CERIANTHARIA

This order covers the burrowing or tube "anemones". They are poorly suited to the reef tank. They have no foot and must be wedged into position somewhere, are lethal to small fishes and shrimps and liable to release toxins if disturbed. A pity, because they are spectacular, with a "fountain" of fine tentacles in pastel colors. They belong in tanks on their own or with other sessile creatures.

ZOANTHIDEA

Another order of anemone-like cnidarians, the zoanthids have a double ring of tentacles and share a common base. Colonies spread around the tank and vary in size of polyps. *Palythoa* is a colorful genus, others are very plain. Some genera have zooxanthellae while others may need to be fed. Some get along on what's around in the water.

CORALLIMORPHARIA

The reef tank has seen a rise of interest in this order. It offers many colorful and attractive forms, hardy and reproducing readily. Most have zooxanthellae and some respond to bright light by developing various colors although originally a dull

The spectacular coral *Catalaphyllia plicata* is a pale, almost white, version of the greenish *C. jardinei*. Both do well in the reef aquarium if the water chemistry is kept under control. Photo by Dr. C. W. Emmens.

brown. In the shade, they fade away again, even becoming white. The blue and red forms are the most popular, particularly blues under actinic light. They can be kept in close contact with one another and may need pruning when too many develop.

Species with fluffy tentacles like *Ricordia*, or knobbly ones like *Rhodactis*, may be quite small or up to 15cm (6") across. They are commonly called mushroom anemones. Others, with almost no tentacles but flat leathery discs can grow even larger. These are the elephant or leather corals in genera like *Actinodiscus* and *Paradiscosoma*. All may catch prey of quite a large size, closing up on it like an anemone. Those, the majority, with zooxanthellae need no food in bright light.

CHAPTER 5
Arthropoda, Echinodermata and Others

The jointed-limbed animals are in an enormous phylum, Arthropoda. It includes insects, spiders, mites, crustaceans and more. Marine forms are almost confined to the class Crustacea. There are a few marine insects. In class Merostomata are the horseshoe crabs. In class Pycnogonida are the sea spiders, but they are not really spiders. The phylum is distinguished by its jointed appendages, the formation of an outer or exoskeleton and the consequent need for molting at intervals. Another feature is segmentation - the division of the body into a series of segments, each typically bearing appendages. These may be jaws, antennae, legs, gills or swimmerets.

Malacostraca
SHRIMPS

Most of the crustaceans of interest to aquarists are in this subclass. The order Decapoda covers the ten-legged crabs, shrimps, lobsters and prawns. Family Stenopodidae includes the coral shrimps. The genus *Stenopus* contains the well-known cleaner shrimps. White feelers tell fishes that this is a cleaner shrimp—let it do its job. *S. hispidus*, with claws like a scorpion, grows to about 8cm (3") and is usually found in pairs. The pair really look after each other. They guard the molting partner and the male feeds the female - not vice versa. They are belligerent to other pairs and will kill small shrimps. The golden cleaner, *S. scutellatus*, and the ghost cleaner, *S. pyrsonatus*, are similar species, the latter being very pale with a red dorsal stripe. All live for several years - not many shrimps do.

There are other cleaners. The genus *Lysmata* is also long lived and can be kept in

Many colorful
species of
Periclimenes,
such as this *P.
yucatanicus*,
inhabit anemones
and corals. Photo
by M. Mesgleski.

The banded coral shrimp, *Stenopus hispidus*, is one of the shrimp most commonly kept in aquaria. Though large and sometimes belligerent, they are easy to keep and occasionally spawn. Photo by Dr. P. Colin.

numbers. It is a bit shyer than *Stenopus,* particularly *L. debelius,* a deep-water beauty. *L. grabhami* is the best known, with two red stripes dorsally. *L. amboinensis* is much like it, but has a red tail as well. The family Palaemonidae has some cleaners - *Periclimenes pedersoni* lives on anemones, leaves them to clean a fish and scuttles back again.

Others of the family live with sponges, sea urchins, corals and gorgonians. Most are dull, not cleaners and short lived. A few nicely colored species are *P. psamathi*, blue and orange, *P. cornutus*, brown and yellow, *P. brevicarpalis*, with colorless males and larger colored females and *P. colemani*, redspotted. They live respectively on gorgonians, sea urchins, anemones and again on sea urchins. You may get any of them as a bonus when buying the host species.

The harlequin shrimp, *Hymenocera picta*, family Gnathophyllidae, is a beauty but feeds on the tube feet of starfishes. It is alleged to eat other meaty foods if tube feet are not available. The genus *Gnathophyllum,*

bumble bee shrimps, has a number of very attractive and harmless species.

Hinge-beak shrimps are in only one genus, *Rhynchocinetes*. They are often capable of color changes, so that the nice red shrimp you bought yesterday is now white. The dancing shrimp, *R. uritai,* is said to be a coral eater, so beware. Hump-backed shrimps, family Hippolytidae, are often very attractive. Some live on cnidarians or sponges. They tend to have a spidery appearance with long bristly legs. Snapping shrimps, family Alpheidae, have many genera. They make a loud cracking noise with an enlarged claw. If one grows up undetected in your tank you may think it has a cracked glass. Some, such as *Alpheus armatus*, are brightly colored.

LOBSTERS AND CRABS

The crayfishes (spiny lobsters) and lobsters tend to get too big for comfort but can often be tolerated for a year or so if bought very small. There are hundreds of species, some very colorful. Oddly only one species of lobster, *Enoplometopus orientalis*, and three species of crayfish, genus *Panulirus*, are found on the Great Barrier reef. The lobster is bright red and grows to about 8". One of the crayfishes, *P. versicolor*, is really beautiful - blue and gold with long white antennae. Americans would call it a spiny lobster, of which they have many species. Some, such as *Justitia longimanus*, are quite decorative.

The squat lobsters, family Galatheidae, are really crabs, belonging to the same group as the hermit crabs. All have either soft abdomens or one that is tucked under the carapace. Most species of squat lobster are small and live on feather stars. The hermit crabs, superfamily Paguroidea, tuck a soft abdomen into univalve mollusc shells. *Paguritta harmsi* and a few others live in calcareous worm tubes. There are many species, and small ones can be tolerated in the reef tank. Large ones are too much of a nuisance.

Attractive genera are *Calcinus*, all with blue eyes and various body colors, and *Paguristes* and *Trizopagurus*, with flattened bodies that fit

cone shells. Avoid the attractive large species often on sale.

The family of porcelain crabs, Porcellanidae, is another group that lives with anemones, sponges, etc. Mostly quite small, they are debris or filter feeders and nice to keep. *Neopetrolisthes* lives with giant anemones and sometimes comes as a welcome extra when you buy one.

True crabs are often unwelcome guests that grow up from tiny specimens in living rock and then are very hard to catch. They should be sought out before adding the rock to the tank. Most are a great nuisance as they grow and strip the scenery. We need to choose carefully which crabs, if any, we wish to have in the aquarium. Families of interest are the Dromiidae, decorator crabs, the Grapsidae, shore crabs, the Calappidae, box and sand crabs, Majidae, spider crabs, and Xanthidae, coral crabs. Each has some suitable members.

The decorator crabs peel off sponges, algae and other things from the rocks and cover their bodies with them. They hold them in position with the two rear

A colorful spider crab. When small, crabs often can be kept in the aquarium, but large specimens can cause disasters. Photo by M. Mesgleski.

The bullseye coral lobster, *Enoplometopus holthuisi*, can be kept in a large aquarium. Seldom aggressive, they may attempt to take the occasional sleeping fish now and then. Photo by S. Johnson.

pairs of legs. Attractive genera are *Petalomera* and *Dromidiopsis*, plus others. The shore crabs, most of which are intertidal, include *Planes minutus*, the sargassum crab. Other suitable genera are *Hemigrapsus* and *Pachygrapsus*, except that they tend to eat macroalgae. The box and sand crabs include the calico crab, *Hepatus epheliticus*, but the rest are bizarre rather than pretty, and liable to eat your favorite molluscs. Small spider crabs such as the arrow crab, *Stenorhynchus seticornis*, are acceptable in the aquarium. It has very long legs and eats debris. Most of the others get far too big.

The coral crabs deserve a paragraph to themselves. Some, such as the brightly colored genus *Trapezia*, live on coral. Others utilize anemones, either covering themselves with them as does the teddy bear crab, *Polydectus cupulifer*, or holding one in each claw, as does *Lybia tesselata*. *Lybia* uses the anemones to catch edible material. Avoid the ugly, dark and hairy xanthids with black tips to the claws that eat up live rock and in some cases are poisonous. Even wrasses, normally very fond of crabs, will not touch them.

MANTIS SHRIMPS

These, together with the unwanted xanthid crabs, are the main creatures to remove carefully from living rock when it is new. They are all dangerous and some can grow to 30cm (1 ft) long. Each has a pair of razor sharp claws held like a praying mantis, with which it can rip up prey, including fishes. A great pity because some of them are very decorative.

OTHER CRUSTACEANS

Various further members of the subclass Malacostraca are the tiny inhabitants of many reef aquaria - there by accident. These are the mysid shrimps, isopods and amphipods, including the skeleton shrimps that climb around algae. Most are quite harmless and good food for fishes.

Copepods, in the subclass Copepoda, are sometimes a nuisance and also have parasitic members. Most are tiny and harmless. *Argulus*, subclass Branchiura, is an important but infrequent parasite of fishes. It is mostly to be found on sea horses and can be removed with forceps. Barnacles, subclass Cirripedia, are aberrant crustaceans that settle head downwards and fish with their feet. They do not usually survive for long in the aquarium. Some are parasites, the most famous being *Sacculina carcini*, which invades the shore crab *Carcinus maenas*. It virtually fills the crab with parasitic tissue and eventually kills it. The well known brine shrimp, *Artemia salina*, is only mentioned because we introduce it into the aquarium as food. It is not really a marine crustacean but lives in strong brine in salt works or in very salty water.

ECHINODERMATA

The echinoderms have a five-fold symmetry in the adults, although they start off with a bilateral symmetry in the larvae. They are believed to be the closest invertebrate phylum to the Chordata - our own phylum. Their greatest peculiarity is the possession of tube feet controlled by a hydraulic water vascular system. With these, they move around and sometimes breathe and feed. They are divided into the following five classes.

ASTEROIDEA

Sea stars always start with five arms but often grow more. They have calcified plates that may make some species quite hard to the touch while others remain soft. There is a mouth below and an anus on top in the central disc. Many are predatory on molluscs or corals but others make good reef tank inhabitants. Some tend to strip live rock while others, like the popular blue star, *Linckia laevigata*, seem to live for years on nothing.

There are many colorful small species. The biscuit star, *Tosia queenslandensis*, is red and yellow with very short arms while the genera *Oreaster*, *Fromia* and *Neoferdina* offer pink, red and yellow species, all attractive. For safety, go for small, flat species as the solid, chunky ones are liable to die and pollute the tank. Then watch carefully to see that you haven't bought a killer!

Choriaster is a so-called "soft" starfish in which the hard plates cover only a part of the animal's body. Soft starfishes often exude mucus when disturbed. Photo by C. Church.

Though starfishes can be major predators in the aquarium, many hobbyists consider their often bright colors to be a plus. Notice the commensal shrimp on this red starfish. Photo by C. Church.

OPHIUROIDEA

Brittle stars have a small central disc and long, slender motile arms. The tube feet serve a respiratory function and movement is by the arms alone. There is no anus, only a mouth, and the majority of species are filter feeders or debris feeders. Some are predatory, large and tough and without the fragility of the rest. Genera such as *Ophiarachna* and *Ophiarachnella* have colorful members that rush out for food, coiling an arm or arms around a chunk of it and retiring rapidly. Small genera live under rocks and are rarely seen, while others swim around actively and settle on rocks or coral.

The genera *Astrophyton* and *Gorgonocephalus* are examples of the basket stars, with repeatedly branching arms forming a tangle acting as a net. They catch planktonic prey and are not for the home aquarium as they will collect up shrimps and even small fishes.

ECHINOIDEA

Imagine a sea star with its arms folded up over its head, tube feet outwards, and then joined into a sphere and you have a sea urchin. The anus is still on top, having migrated up through the center of the animal. In addition to the tube feet, there are rows of pedicellariae, small nippers, and of spines. The pedicellariae are also seen in some sea stars, but not the spines. Movement is by both tube feet and spines.

Small, short-spined urchins are suitable for aquaria, feeding on encrusting algae, detritus or dead animals. Some are a bit too thorough and strip living rock but most can be tolerated. Attractive genera are numerous - *Eucidaris*, *Prionocidaris*, *Tripneustes* and *Mespilia*, etc. Avoid *Asthenosoma* with poisonous spines. Sea urchins do not all acclimatize readily to the aquarium and are not always available in pet shops.

HOLOTHUROIDEA

Sea cucumbers are soft-bodied, usually elongated, sausage-shaped echinoderms. Imagine a sea star fused as in the sea urchins and then pulled out with a mouth and tentacles in front and an anus behind. Only tube feet remain and

Bright blue is not a common color in the aquarium with few fishes, thus the value of the blue starfish *Linckia laevigata*. Photo by Dr. C. W. Emmens.

Mediaster aequalis is not only bright red, but it clearly shows the fascinating pattern of small plates so typical of the body of starfishes. Photo by D. Wrobel.

Two of the odder starfishes. Above, *Oreaster*, a chocolate chip starfish; below, *Culcita*, a pincushion star. Photos by A. Mancini (above) and M. & C. Piednoir.

the typical cucumber sifts through sand extracting what nourishment it can. A few are decorative but others can be useful as cleaners if you have a sandy bottom to the tank. Otherwise they will be pretty unhappy. If annoyed they also throw out long sticky threads from the anus. These are poisonous and death to small creatures that get entangled in them.

So stick to small specimens if you decide to keep them. Decorative genera are *Holothuria, Bohadschia* and *Cucumaria,* the latter being a filter feeder.

The family Dendrochirotidae has the most beautiful filter feeders of all. Generally known as sea apples, they sit upright, perched on rocks or any firm support. Species such as *Paracucumaria tricolor* are really spectacular, with in *P. tricolor,* a blue body, red tube feet and bright red, white and blue branching tentacles. Each tentacle is thrust into the mouth in turn, wiping off whatever it has caught. To keep them is risky, as they can exude a potent toxin if unhappy or if they die. They are so stunning that small specimens are often kept despite the risk. If reef tank conditions are well maintained, the risk is quite small.

CRINOIDEA

Feather stars are the remnants of a much larger phylum in the past. Sea lilies were a dominant echinoderm millions of years ago, but are now found only in deep water. Their stalk

Left: The urchin *Sphaerechinus granularis*, showing pedicellariae around the mouth. Photo by M. & C. Piednoir. Below: The brittle star *Ophiothrix suensenii* on a sponge. Photo by C. Church.

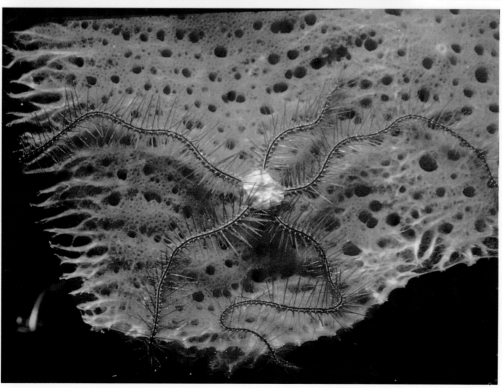

Sea urchins.
Right: An edible
urchin,
Tripneustes.
Photo by C.
Church. Below: A
very spiny
Echinometra.
Photo by C. Platt.

Sea cucumbers. Left: *Holothuria*, one of the types sometimes called sea apples. Photo by A. Norman. Below: The colorful filter feeder *Cucumaria insolens* of South Africa. Photo by Dr. T. E. Thompson.

persists throughout life but is soon discarded by the developing feather star. It then swims around by its feathery arms, up to fifty of them in some species. It is unfortunate that the arms get nipped by fishes and others so that the feather stars rarely do well in the aquarium. They are very colorful, in red, yellow, green, black and purple, etc., often striped as well. Small prey are caught by the arms and swept to the mouth by cilia and mucus. Claspers on the base of the central disc enable their owner to hold onto algae or corals.

There are many genera. The antedonids and tropiometrids have several each, all with ten arms. *Comactinea* hides all day but *Analcidometra* swims around gracefully. The comasterids have more arms and a great range of sizes and colors and are visible by day if not very active.

MOLLUSCA

This phylum is to some extent neglected by aquarists but offers a wide selection of good aquarium species. Many of them are useful too, eating hair algae, cleaning up debris and cleaning the aquarium glass. Others are filter feeders while yet others are dangerous predators. Peculiar to them, but not universal, is the possession of a radula, a long file-like tongue that can rasp away at food. The secretion of a shell by an organ, the mantle, is also characteristic of molluscs, again not universal.

Feather stars often are found resting on the reef edge, feeding in the currents. Photo by M. & C. Piednoir.

POLYPLACOPHORA

The chitons are primitive molluscs with eight dorsal, flexible plates and a large foot. They can roll up like a woodlouse if pried from a rock on which they have a home site. Most are algae eaters and useful scavengers, some quite colorful. The genera *Acanthopleura* and *Lucilina* are typical. The black chiton, *Katharina truncata,* has a girdle that almost covers the dorsal plates. Most chitons are blind, but some have a shell studded with eyes, hundreds in *Schizochiton incisus!*

GASTROPODA

This is the class of snails, the "stomach-footed" molluscs. Most secrete shells and have a head with eyes, mouth, etc. and a hind end that may be twisted around to lie beside it. Beside the popular cowries there are dozens of desirable species for the reef tank. Useful and decorative species include the tropical

When detached from the reef, feather stars swim by using all their arms. Most species are very fragile and hard to maintain. Photo by M. & C. Piednoir.

Top shells, *Calliostoma*, are brilliant, exquisitely shaped snails that graze on algae. The jeweled top shell, *C. annulatum*, of California (bottom) is especially attractive. Photos by C. Platt.

abalones, *Haliotis*, smaller and more colorful than the table species from cooler waters. *Trochus, Calliostoma, Tectus* and *Astraea* are all useful genera and quite attractive.

Genera to be avoided are the sundial shells, *Architectonia, Heliacus*, etc., which feed on zoanthids and other small cnidarians. Also the carnivorous whelks, family Buccinidae, tritons, family Cymatiidae, murex shells, family Muricidae,

volutes, family Volutidae and quite a number of other families are all carnivores, eating other molluscs in many cases.

Cone shells and turrid shells, families Conidae and Turridae, are poisonous in addition. They have a hollow spine at the end of the radula that injects poison into their prey - fishes, gastropods and other invertebrates. They can give you a nasty wound and have been known to kill humans.

Also grazing on algae (and sometimes on sponges and bryozoans) are the cowries, more appreciated by shell collectors than by aquarists. This is *Cypraea zebra*, the Caribbean measled cowry. Photo by C. Church.

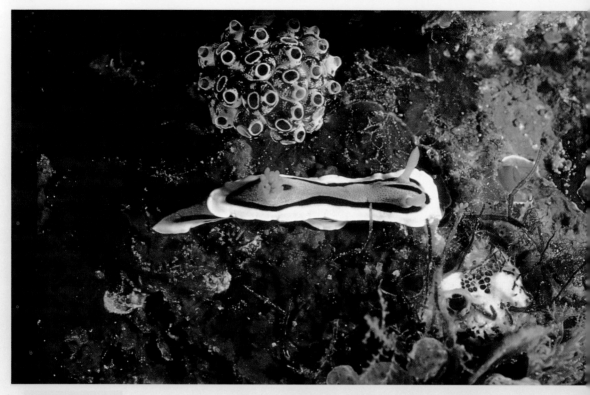

The subclass Opisthobranchia has reduced or absent shells, from the bubble-shells to the nudibranchs. The sea hares, family Aplysiidae, are algae eaters and make useful aquarium species, although they can grow too large; they are easily removed. The nudibranchs are all carnivores with mostly special feeding habits. A great pity since they are very decorative, but as they almost always starve to death, they should not be kept. Most of them feed on a particular invertebrate, not just a sponge, tube worm or bryozoan but only on a particular species. The suborder Doridacea is the nearest to an exception, as some will eat a variety of foods.

BIVALVIA
This is the class of mussels, oysters, etc. with two halves to the shell, hinged together by an elastic

Although nudibranchs such as this *Chromodoris* are colorful, they seldom survive long in the aquarium lacking the sponges and bryozoans necessary to feed them. Photo by C. Church.

Left: The flamingo tongue snail, *Cyphoma gibbosum*, feeds only upon living sea fans. Photo by C. Church. Below: *Hermissenda crassicornis*, a nudibranch from the tropical East Pacific. Photo by C. Platt.

Right: The flame scallop, *Lima scabra*. Photo by C. Platt. Below: A colorful *Glossodoris* nudibranch. Photo by C. Church.

110

ligament. They have no head, no radula and are filter feeders, sometimes supplemented by zooxanthellae as in clams. Many species have a byssus, a mass of threads tying them to a substrate. Others have a foot and can move around, often in sand or mud. Scallops, *Pecten,* etc., can flap their shells and blow water from the exhalant siphon to cruise up into the water. Some are attractively colored and command the attention of the aquarist. The so-called flame scallop, *Lima scabra,* is actually a file-shell, family Limidae. True scallops, family Pectinidae, may have nicely colored shells. The genus *Chlamys* is the most attractive.

The giant clams, family Tridacnidae, are aquarium favorites, the genera *Tridacna* and *Hippopus* having zooxanthellae. The mantle is often brightly colored and patterned. They must be in good light, and it seems to be a general finding that they do best in metal halide lighting. Giant

Giant clams, *Tridacna,* have become popular aquarium subjects in the last few years. Many are farmed in the South Pacific. Photo by C. Church.

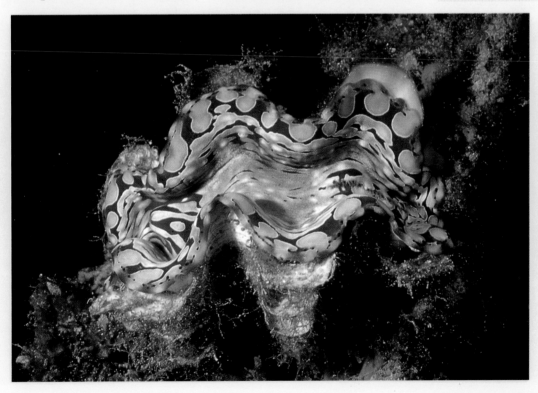

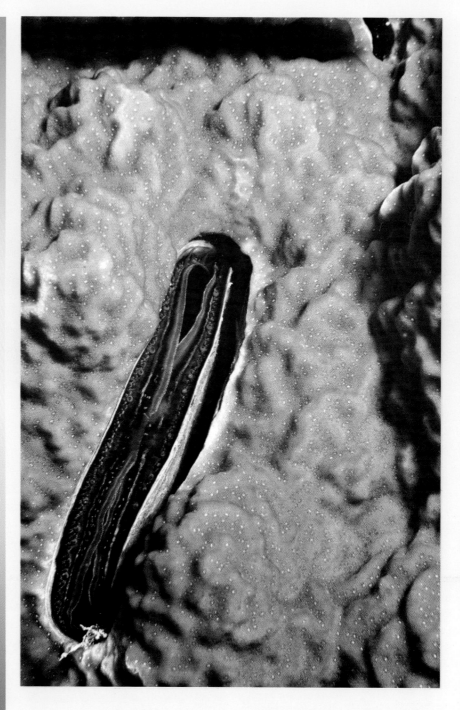

Pedum is an unusual and colorful scallop that lives in burrows within coral heads. The bright red spots are its "eyes." Photo by S. Johnson.

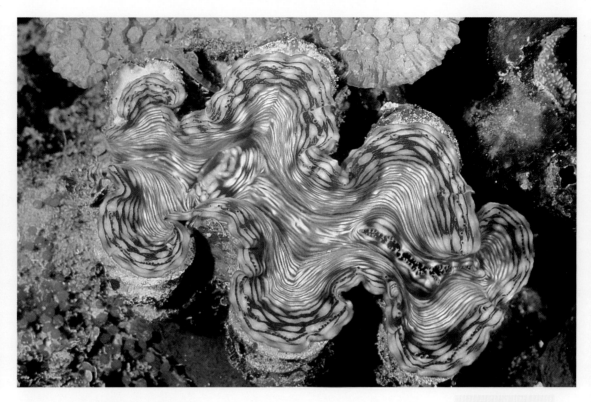

clams are the largest reef molluscs known and are not for the aquarium. Suitable species such as *T. crocea* only grow to about 15cm (6"). Some other reef bivalves are worth having, such as the sunset clams, family Psammobiidae. They are rarely offered but may grow up from living rock.

CEPHALOPODA

Octopuses, squids and nautilus - quite unsuited to a reef tank!

WORMS

You are going to have more worms in your reef tank than any other creatures except microbes. Most of them can only be seen with a lens or microscope. They belong to a number of phyla of which the nematodes are commonest. It is said that if I became the invisible man you could still see me as a ghostly apparition because of my cloak of them. Nice thought.

Most species of giant clams have "windows" in the mantle that admit sunlight. Symbiotic algae use this light to produce sugars and starches in turn used by the clam, which does not have to actively feed. Photo by C. Church.

Feather duster worms. Right: *Branchioma*. Photo by C. Platt. Below: *Spirographis*. Photo by M. & C. Piednoir.

114

I shall start however with worms you are likely to want to see. Some are very decorative and make good reef tank inhabitants. First and foremost are the annelids, phylum Annelida, divided into two classes, Polychaeta and Oligochaeta. The polychaetes are mostly marine but the oligochaetes are mostly freshwater or on land, so we shall forget them.

POLYCHAETA

The segmented, many-bristled worms have typically a head with eyes, jaws, tentacles and antennae. Each segment has a pair of legs and maybe gills. But those most seen by the aquarist live in tubes and have a very different structure. The feather duster worms, family Sabellidae, build membranous tubes attached to rocks or coral from which an often colored crown of tentacles emerges. The crown of a large species like *Sabella pavonia* may be 10cm (4") across, striped with red, orange or brown or

115

just a solid color.

The families Serpulidae and Spirorbidae build limey tubes and are mostly smaller than the sabellids. The popular *Spirobranchus giganteus*, the Christmas tree worm, isn't very gigantic but is very colorful. There may be blue, red, orange, brown, white or variegated wormheads on one piece of rock. The genus *Spirorbis* forms coiled tubes on a rock

The paired tentacle crowns of *Spirobranchus* are characteristic, as is the screw-stepped pattern of the tentacles around their base. Photo above by G. Spies, on left by C. Church.

surface and is never so colorful.

Chaetopterus variopedatus, family Chaetopteridae, is a worm that constructs a U-shaped tube about 30cm (1 ft) in length. The tube is parchment-like and so the worm is invisible, but you can make a suitable glass tube and put the worm into it. It is a typical polychaete in shape but not in its habits. In the tube, it beats modified legs to make a current that flows through a sheet of mucus that catches prey. The worm is also luminous and glows blue if the tube is tapped in the dark.

The clam and lug worms, family Nereidae, pass masses of sand through their gut and are familiar as bait. *Arenicola* also builds a U-shaped tube but is not transferable to glass and is not a filter feeder. In genera like *Eunice,* the palolo worm, swarming for reproduction occurs at certain seasons, when the worms, or segments of them, swim to the surface. Just mentioned for interest!

The family of scale worms, Polynoidae, is famous for the sea mouse, *Aphrodita*. It is a solid oval worm about the

Large, free-living worms often are dangerous to both the corals in the tank and to the keeper. The spines of both *Aphrodita*, the sea mouse (top), and *Hermodice carunculata*, the Caribbean fire worm, can cause painful stings. Photo at top by A. Kerstitch, at bottom by D. Reed.

Eurythoe is the common Indo-Pacific fire worm. Divers avoid contact with it because of the powerful stinging actions of its spines. It feeds on living coral polyps. Photo by C. Platt.

size of a mouse, mostly hidden under rocks. In the open, clear of sand or debris, it is a quite spectacular sight. The sea mouse will live in the aquarium on debris and bits of various fish foods. Some species are poisonous and must be handled with care.

More slender and worm-like are the fire worms, family Amphinomidae, found in coral. They too have poisonous bristles (setae) that pierce the skin and break off when touched. They can be a great source of trouble in the aquarium, hidden by day and emerging by night to cause devastation.

PLATYHELMINTHES

The phylum of flatworms includes flukes and tapeworms, but some of the free-living members, class Turbellaria, are quite decorative. However, they are mostly carnivores, feeding on molluscs or other worms. Various *Pseudoceros* species, up to 5cm (2") long, are colorful and swim into

There are many colorful but poorly known swimming flatworms. This is *Pseudoceros bedfordi*. Photo by K. Gillett.

Bugula neritina, one of the most common types of bryozoans. Photo by K. Lucas.

the water. They are nasty tasting and rarely eaten by fishes. Other genera are similar, often unidentified and coming with living rock. Other worm phyla are of interest as fish foods or parasites. They include the nematodes already mentioned, rotifers and peanut worms that live in coral.

OTHER PHYLA

The phylum Bryozoa provides many genera of minute filter feeders that encrust wharf piling, rocks and seaweeds, even ships' hulls. Some are calcified; others, like *Bugula,* are soft and wave around like an alga. *Membranipora* species are very pretty and form colorful colonies. Phylum Entoprocta closely resembles bryozoans in appearance but is structurally quite different.

The phylum Brachiopoda, lamp shells, mimics bivalve molluscs in appearance. It is related to the two phyla above in having a peculiar feeding organ, the lophophore, surrounding the mouth. It traps particles in mucus and passes them to the mouth. The brachiopods are

Two delicate sea squirts. The species at the top is *Diazona violacea*. Photo at top by M. & C. Piednoir, at bottom by C. Platt.

123

sometimes found in the aquarium on rocks or seaweeds and are usually mistaken for molluscs.

The phylum Chordata is of course represented in the sea by the fishes and some mammals. But it has other members that come as a surprise to most people. The Tunicata, or sea squirts and others, are a good example. The larval stages have a notochord, an elastic rod that becomes the backbone of vertebrates. They also have gill slits, the two items together placing them in the phylum. Various sea squirts survive if lucky in reef tanks, but many gradually degenerate. They are filter feeders and most of them do not like bright light. They must therefore feed on particles or minute organisms in the water and mostly do not get enough. Do not try to make up for this by using invertebrate food or you will probably foul the tank.

CHAPTER 6
Fishes for the Reef Aquarium

Most of us like to keep a few fishes in the miniature reef tank. They add brisk movement to the scenery and some of them can perform useful tasks such as keeping algae down. However, we must remember that they add to the burden of the tank, being producers of pollution and taking nothing away from it. So, not too many should be introduced. These must also be carefully selected since we do not want the scenery devastated or precious invertebrates eaten. Neither do we want to house specimens that will jump out of an uncovered aquarium or those that are unhappy because the environment is all wrong for them. It is best also to keep to fishes that will not grow

Triggerfishes, such as this *Oxymonacanthus longirostris*, tend to be aggressive and nippy in the aquarium. Photo by M. & C. Piednoir.

125

too large since removing them from a reef aquarium can involve a lot of strife and is likely to wreck the setup.

UNWANTED FISHES

Unless you want no algae to survive, except for encrusting types, the general run of surgeons (Acanthuridae) must be omitted. They also mostly grow fast and large. The exceptions are dealt with below. Large angels (Pomacanthidae) or their juveniles are also out since they not only grow big but many feed on corals and small shrimps, etc. Chaetodons are to be omitted for similar reasons, even those that do not grow large. Wrasses love crabs and other crustaceans and would also miss deep sand in which to burrow. Triggerfishes (Balistidae) are too belligerent and also like to feed on various invertebrates. Since most of the fishes kept will be quite small, predators are not welcome except in very

Large surgeonfishes, such as *Paracanthurus hepatus*, are dangerous algae-eaters in the reef aquarium. Photo by M. & C. Piednoir.

special circumstances that will be discussed later.

WHAT'S LEFT?

Luckily, plenty of attractive and compatible fishes. They are best dealt with in family groups.

POMACENTRIDAE

Here is a vast array of mostly small fishes including the anemonefishes and damsels. They are tough, colorful and often aggressive, being very territorial, particularly when guarding eggs. However, they mostly object to other similar fishes and will leave the majority of tank-mates alone. Even when they attack, they rarely do severe damage. An exception commonly on sale is *Dascyllus trimaculatus*, the three-spot damselfish, which is liable to grow big and fierce. Another exception is *Premnas biaculeatus*, the spine-cheeked anemonefish; the females in particular

Colorful anemonefishes and a humbug damselfish. Top to bottom: *Amphiprion nigripes* (photo by R. Steene) *Amphiprion sebae* (photo by Dr. G. R. Allen); *Dascyllus aruanus* (photo by R. Steene).

127

Top: The three-spot damselfish, *Dascyllus trimaculatus*. Photo by Dr. G. R. Allen. Bottom: *Premnas biaculeatus,* the spine-cheeked anemonefish. Photo by M. & C. Piednoir.

Two anemonefishes on their anemones. Top: *Amphiprion bicinctus* on *Entacmaea*. Photo by G. Spies. Bottom: *Amphiprion clarkii* on *Heteractis*. Photo by J. Carlen.

grow too large and combative.

A favorite sight is a group of anemonefishes with their large tropical anemone. If one is not available, they will adapt to a coral such as *Goniopora* or *Catalaphyllia*. The appearance of two adults with a family of young is misleading. They are all fishes of about the same age, two of which are a male and a female whose secretions (pheromones) keep the others juvenile and small. If the female dies, the male becomes a female and one of the others becomes a male. They will frequently breed, laying groups of eggs under the anemone at about two-week intervals.

GOBIIDAE AND BLENNIIDAE

These constitute another large selection of mostly harmless little fishes, some gloriously colored and a few very useful eaters of hair algae, such as the *Ecsenius* and *Salarius* blennies. It is a pity that many of them are not more commonly available; genera such as *Enneanectes*, for instance, offer some 1½" beauties. The well-known neon goby, *Gobiosoma oceanops*, is a cleaner like some others, while many species have developed commensal habits with shrimps, sea urchins and corals.

The genera *Ptereleotris* and *Nemateleotris* (fire fishes) have some fabulous free-swimming members that are unfortunately jumpers and so must be kept tightly covered. *N. magnifica* and *N. decora* are especially colorful, but beware of cyanide-caught

The small but colorful blenny *Ecsenius axelrodi* feeds at least in part on hair algae. Photo by R. Steene.

The delicately colored neon gobies *Gobiosoma oceanops* (top) and *Gobiosoma randalli* (center) contrast greatly with the fire fish *Nemateleotris magnifica*, yet all are fine aquarium additions. Photos of *Gobiosoma* by W. Starck, that of *Nemateleotris* by Dr. H. R. Axelrod.

specimens that die in a few weeks. Incidentally, the genera *Ptereleotris* and *Nemateleotris* are now considered by some to be in the family Microdesmidae.

CALLIONYMIDAE

The dragonets include some beautiful little fishes, the best of which is probably the commonest available - *Pterosynchiropus splendidus*, the mandarin fish. Another, *Synchiropus picturatus*, the green-ring mandarin, is equally attractive but harder to keep. These are benthic, slow moving and slow eating fishes that fare badly in an ordinary community tank, but in a reef tank they find plenty to eat as they forage

Pterosynchiropus splendidus is one of the most colorful and readily available dragonets or mandarin fishes. Photo by M. & C. Piednoir.

at leisure among the rocks and algae. Males fight, but females or a pair can be kept together.

PSEUDOCHROMIDAE

Most of the dottybacks are small, attractive but sometimes rather pugnacious fishes. However, their small size (mostly) renders them fairly harmless. *Pseudochromis porphyreus* and *P. paccagnellae* are favorites and grow only to about 2" long, but there is quite a range of other, less commonly available species. *P. cyanotaenia* and *P.*

Top: The Swissguard, *Liopropoma rubre,* is a colorfui tiny bass that often is available. Photo by Dr. J. Randall. Bottom: The solid bright purple *Pseudochromis fridmani* is not readily available but certainly is one of the most unusual of small fishes. Photo by B. Kahl.

olivaceous are said to be very belligerent, despite their small size.

GRAMMIDAE

The basslets include the well-known royal gramma, *Gramma loreto,* but there are other equally nice species whose only drawback is a tendency to hide. *G. melacara* grows a bit larger than *G. loreto,* to 10cm (4"), and has more purple on the body and no yellow hind parts. Of the lot of them, only *Assessor macneilli* is said to be combative.

SERRANIDAE

This is the family of sea basses and groupers, with members of enormous size, whose juveniles are nevertheless sometimes kept until they grow too large. Not for the reef tank, as it may be too difficult to get them out again. There are however the subfamilies of Anthiinae and a few others that stay small and make interesting pets. There are various species of *Anthias*, most of them colorful and fairly small, that swim in mid-water, preferably in small shoals. *Pseudanthias squamipinnis*, one of the first kept, can be yellow, purple or even bluish

The royal gramma or fairy basslet, *Gramma loreto,* is perhaps the most strikingly colored fish available for the home aquarium. Photo by C. Church.

in color. The colors of most other species are mixtures of yellow and red. The genus *Mirolabrichthys* offers a similar range of somewhat slimmer fishes.

Most *Serranus* species stay small and are bottom dwellers. They offer a nice variety of barred and spotted fishes, many of them from American tropical waters. Some are unfortunately unsuitable because of pugnacity, and it is wise to consult appropriate authorities or books before a purchase. More of the genus *Liopropoma* are peaceful and small and also bottom dwellers. Their only drawback is a decided preference for live foods. The hamlets, *Hypoplectrus,* come in various colors that may in fact be only varieties of a single species. As they are pugnacious they are best avoided, unless with larger fishes. They grow to about 10-13cm (4"-5"). Don't be fooled by *Cromileptes altivelis,* the leopard grouper, often on sale at 5-8cm (2"-3") and looking most attractive. It is a killer and grows to 75cm (2½ ft). The same for *Grammistes sexlineatus,* which loves feeding on small fishes and grows to 30cm (1 ft).

Anthiids are colorful, usually small schooling basses mostly from the Indo-Pacific. Top: *Mirolabrichthys dispar*. Photo by A. Powers. Bottom: *Pseudanthias pleurotaenia*. Photo by R. Myers.

PLESIOPIDAE

The most attractive members of this family do not stay small, but are so beautiful that you may wish to keep one of them. They hide away at night as do most other fishes, so if they grow too large it is difficult to catch them out from a reef tank. *Calloplesiops altivelis* and *C. argus*, the comet fishes, grow to about 15cm (6"), which is usually tolerable, and are only belligerent towards their own kind.

Paraplesiops meleagris, another comet, gets to 25cm (10"), but is so lovely that I'd risk it! It is bright blue. All are spotted long-finned beauties that will take dry foods and will also swallow tiny fishes, so be warned!

HAEMULIDAE

A family mentioned for the same reason as above - fishes that grow big but can be caught out easily, swimming around at night. *Plectorhinchus chaetodonoides*, the clown

Though colorful and readily available, hamlets (such as this *Hypoplectrus guttavarius*) tend to be aggressive. Photo by C. Church.

Top: Few fish can compare with the juvenile jackknife high-hat, *Equetus lanceolatus;* even adults are high-finned and colorful. Photo by Dr. J. Randall. Bottom: The comet fish *Calloplesiops altivelis* is strikingly colored, but beware of the large mouth. Photo by A. Spreinat.

Heniochus acuminatus often is called the banner butterflyfish. Several butterflyfishes have high dorsal fins, stay small, and feed well in the reef aquarium. Photo by M. & C. Piednoir.

sweetlips, is a nice-looking peaceful fish, but less attractive as it grows up to 60cm (2 ft). *P. albovittatus* is also nice when young, but grows to 20cm (8"). Both dislike dry foods, but will take frozen foods of all kinds.

SCIAENIDAE

Juvenile high-hats, *Equetus* spp., are often kept in aquaria, but grow to 25cm (10") and are therefore rather unsuitable for any but large reef tanks. If you want a pennant-type fish,

one of the genus *Heniochus* would be more suitable, as they swim up into the water more and also don't grow quite as big. Don't try Moorish idols, *Zanclus canescens*, unless you are a very experienced aquarist.

LABRIDAE

Most wrasses are out of the question; they get too large and eat crustaceans, often also being rather unhappy without deep sand in which to burrow. The most suitable are the cleaners, genus *Labroides*, of which *L. dimidiatus* is the most frequently seen. They continue the cleaning habit often shown by juvenile fishes into adult life and perform a useful job in the aquarium. Get two so that they can clean each other.

It is a pity about the wrasses because some are very attractive fishes, often changing colors spectacularly as they grow up. But they are hard to catch even in a normal aquarium and any that grow large must be avoided. The genus *Cirrhilabrus* has many

Cleaner wrasses, *Labroides dimidiatus* (here cleaning another wrasse, *Novaculichthys taeniourus*), are colorful small fish that do well in the aquarium. Photo by B. Kahl.

Top: *Cirrhilabrus jordani*, one of the smaller and more colorful wrasses. Photo by M. & C. Piednoir. Bottom: *Centropyge acanthops,* one of the most stunning of the pygmy angelfishes. Photo by R. Lubbock.

species that are colorful and stay small, under about 10cm (4"), and so could be tolerated if you don't keep small crustaceans or other live critters that matter. Don't be fooled by *Coris* species, they grow to 30 or 60cm (1 or 2ft long). There are lots of other species and just the odd few stay small. Look up any of them that takes your fancy just in case it isn't too formidable and will not get too large.

POMACANTHIDAE

Most of the pygmy angels, genus *Centropyge*, are suitable but some are rather

Centropyge aurantonotus of the southern Caribbean is one of only two pygmy angelfishes in the western Atlantic. Photo by A. Norman.

An exception among the generally not recommended surgeonfishes is the yellow tang, *Zebrasoma flavescens,* whose bright color and small size make up for other faults. Photo by M. & C. Piednoir.

touchy. This includes *C. bicolor,* the two-colored angelfish, which often does well for a few months in a reef tank and then suddenly dies. However, some of my acquaintances have kept one for over a year. The flame angel, *C. loriculus,* behaves similarly. These angels also tolerate each other badly and can rarely be kept together, even if of different species.

ACANTHURIDAE

The few surgeons that can be safely kept in a reef tank are in fact welcome additions because they eat hair algae and not macroalgae. *Acanthurus pyroferus* and *A. chronixis,* the mimic surgeons, both start off yellow and will swim with yellow surgeons like *Zebrasoma flavescens.* Later they change color, becoming darker and perhaps less attractive - it depends on your preference. They both get to about 18cm (7") and both leave anything but hair algae alone. The genus *Ctenochaetus* has similar habits; *C. strigosus* stays

yellow, but there are darker colored strains that are dark as juveniles. Other *Ctenochaetus* species are variously colored. *C. hawaiiensis* goes from speckled brownish-orange to dark-striped as it grows. They all get to 15-20cm (6-8") in length.

If you don't mind macroalgae being eaten, many other surgeons are peaceful vegetarians, but most of them eventually get too big. *Zebrasoma flavescens* is a nice exception, only growing to 15cm (6"), while *Z. scopas* and *Z. rostratum,* the black surgeons, stay nearly as small. Some of the rabbit fishes, genera *Lo* and *Siganus,* family Siganidae, stay smallish and do no harm and will eat any prepared food.

APOGONIDAE

This is a family of many small species, most of them under 10cm (4") in length and many of them attractive. Their worst habit is a

The pajama cardinalfish, *Sphaeramia nematoptera,* remains the most popular cardinalfish for the reef aquarium. Photo by M. & C. Piednoir.

tendency to hide away during the daytime. So see what any on offer are doing before you buy them. They like their own company and look best in small groups. The most popular, because it swims freely in the water, is *Sphaeramia nematoptera*.

MONODACTYLIDAE

The moonfish or mono, *Monodactylus sebae*, grows rather large, to 20cm (8"), but is interesting as it can be kept in sea water or hard fresh water. Small specimens, preferably several, make a pretty sight in a reef aquarium. A much smaller but quite attractive relative is *Schuettea woodwardi* from cooler waters around Australia, but it can take tropical temperatures. It grows to only 5cm (2").

CENTRISCIDAE

If you can provide suitable food, small live critters such as newly hatched brine shrimp, a group of shrimp fishes is a delight. They swim vertically and like to associate with long-spined sea urchins. *Centriscus scutatus* grows to about 15cm (6") and is the occasionally available species—although not very often!

SYNGNATHIDAE

It is a pity that the most bizarre of the sea horse and pipefish family are so rarely available—the sea dragons. The genus *Solenostomus* is just the right size for a medium to large tank. *S. paradoxus* grows to about 15cm (6") and comes in a variety of colors - red, purplish, black with blue spots, while other species offer further variety. Like the shrimp fishes, they need small live foods, easily supplied as brine shrimp, mosquito wrigglers or copepods. Other sea dragons grow too large and some are open water and cooler water species, but they are spectacular.

"Ordinary" sea horses are weird enough and commonly available, in the genus *Hippocampus*. They are easily kept and bred, but best on their own or with other slow feeders on live foods. You probably know already that the male carries the young in an abdominal pouch, from which they emerge as tiny replicas of

the adult. They can be raised on newly hatched brine shrimp and dwarf species can be kept on them throughout life. Even larger species will survive, but not attain full size, although they will breed and produce fewer young than is normal.

Sea horses range from 5 to 30cm (2" to 12") in size, the more tropical ones being usually the smallest. There are many species and their colors vary both between and within species, from almost white through yellows and reds to black. Some are mottled purplish to blue, but most are just a single color.

There are many species of pipefish, in which males also carry the young. They are all very slender and on the whole less hardy and less attractive than the sea horses.

PREDATORS

Most aquarists prefer to keep the smaller fishes characteristic of the reefs in a reef tank. There is nothing

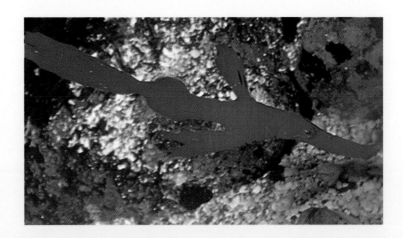

however, against keeping an appropriate number of larger predatory fishes as long as there is no suitable prey as well. Still include only fishes that inhabit reefs or they may get stung by corals or anemones. And, of course, exclude any that will damage the scenery.

The outstanding family of predators, for beauty and ease of keeping, is the Scorpaenidae. It includes the popular lion or turkey fishes, of which *Pterois volitans* is the best known. My own favorite is *P. radiata*, the tail-bar lion fish, but there are many others, grading into the shorter finned but equally poisonous scorpion fishes. All must be handled carefully since the dorsal fin spines have venom glands that can give very painful stings or even kill. In the aquarium, they leave anything they cannot swallow alone and also ignore tiny foods such as brine shrimp except when they are very young. However, they can swallow fishes nearly as large as themselves and so must be with equally large companions. They can be taught to eat chunks of prawn, fish or meat dangled in front of them. If you can keep up a supply of trash fishes, freshwater or saltwater, they will display their hunting skills.

A nice mixture is sea horses and lion fishes of compatible size, since neither is interested in the other's food. The sea horses can hunt their tiny prey while the lion fishes gulp down their own food. Eventually they may grow too big for the sea horses, but a suitable choice of juvenile lions and reasonably large sea horses will last safely for a long time. All are not too difficult to remove from a reef tank when the time comes.

Sea horses, pipefishes and mandarins make another compatible mixture, although not of predators but of slow eaters. Other dragonets than the mandarins can be added if available, although you have to look out for fighting. Usually they bristle up to one another if of different species but do not actually fight. Don't forget that sea horses need something to twine their tails around, which may not be present unless it is provided. If you can't keep staghorn coral alive, put in a few dead pieces.

Another very interesting scene can be of tropical frog or anglerfishes, family

Pterois volitans has a large mouth, tremendous appetite, and venomous fin spines, yet it still is one of the most popular reef fishes. Keep them with equally large fishes. Photo by M. & C. Piednoir.

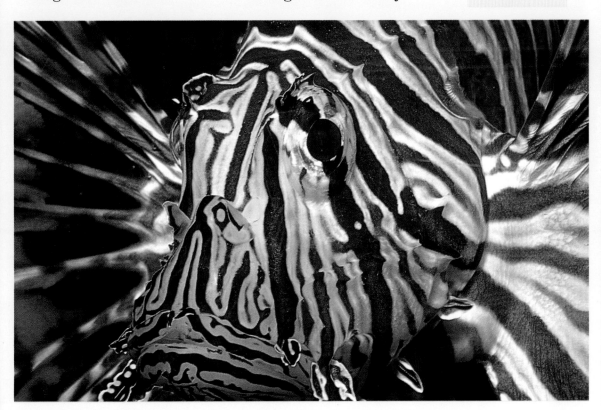

Antennariidae. They will not damage anything they cannot swallow, but like the lion fishes they will devour quite large prey. So they cannot be kept with smaller fishes or crustaceans. These fishes offer a tremendous range of colors and many stay quite small. Species under 10cm (4") include *Antennarius coccineus* (yellow), *A. strigatus* (white), *A. biocellatus* (red), *Tathicarpus butleri* (bluish)

and *A. maculatus* (variegated with white, reds, and yellows).

All of the anglers have a bait of varying size and shape carried on a spine on the nose. In many the bait resembles a tasty worm or even a small fish that is waved in front of the prey. The latter is gulped down with a surprisingly swift movement as it goes to take the bait.

CHAPTER 7
Common Problems

The commonest cause of trouble in reef and many other aquaria is undoubtedly unwanted algae. The word *algae* is used to cover a variety of organisms straddling two kingdoms of living creatures - Bacteria and Protists. It includes the cyanobacteria (blue-green algae), encrusting and hair algae, dinoflagellates (including zooxanthellae), free-living unicellular algae and the many forms of macroalgae (fronded algae with hold-fasts). All can cause grief in the aquarium.

CYANOBACTERIA

The cyanobacteria were the first living things to develop chlorophyll. They were thus able to use the energy of sunlight to manufacture simple sugars from carbon dioxide and water. In nature, they can be a pest in fresh or salt water when excessive nutrients are present. They form dense masses of colored "blooms" that are often toxic, either because they produce poisons or because they use up the available oxygen in the water when they die off.

Way back in the history of the earth, the atmosphere had no oxygen, but a by-product of cyanobacterial activity was the freeing of oxygen gas into the air or water. Organisms that at that time did not use oxygen for respiration found it a deadly poison. They had gradually to evolve ways of dealing with it or to avoid it altogether. Those that learned aerobic respiration (using oxygen) found it much more efficient than their previous methods. It was this that made rapid movement and the development of animals possible. So however much we dislike the cyanobacteria in our aquaria, we should remember that without them we would probably not be here.

These so-called blue-green algae actually come in many colors - brown, yellow, maroon, red and even black, as well as in greens. A maroon variety seems to have spread across the world recently in aquaria, causing lots of trouble. It grows rapidly as sheets or filaments and even increases over night. It can produce moving tips that push up through coral sand. These can been seen to wave around and cover much of a tank and its contents in a few days. In general, cyanobacteria need light, nitrates and phosphates to flourish. So the first things to check are the nitrate and phosphate concentrations. Anything over 5ppm (parts per million) of nitrate-nitrogen and 1ppm of orthophosphate is too much.

The next thing is the dissolved oxygen. That should be near to saturation. The redox potential should be over 400 in the tank and 450 if measured at the pump. Despite the fact that cyanobacteria manufacture oxygen, they do not do well if in too much of it. It will not usually be profitable to reduce the lighting. If other factors are at fault the condition will continue, if more slowly, and return in full when the lights are restored.

The best way to tackle the general problem is to increase the use of protein skimming. It helps to remove pollutants before they become nitrates and phosphates, dragging the oxygen down in the process. The bacteria that effect the conversion use oxygen in the rocks and filters and so lower its concentration in the aquarium. If despite such measures the pest remains, the last resource is an antibiotic. I don't like adding any "cures" to a reef aquarium, but a few days of erythromycin can work. At 50-100mg per gallon it will usually set back cyanobacteria enough to help to get rid of them. Filters will be affected, but a trickle filter can be turned off for most of the time, or entirely separated from the tank and flushed independently. Other antibiotics may prove as effective, but seem not to have been as fully investigated.

HAIR ALGAE

These are subject to the same requirements as cyanobacteria, but flourish at higher redox potentials. Luckily, some fishes will eat them and competition from macroalgae tends to keep them down. Various molluscs can also help, such as the well-known turbo snails, trochus and abalones. So can some sea urchins, but they tend to act like bulldozers and clear up everything before them. These algae-eaters are most effective with short growths of hair algae and they will also remove soft encrusting algae. Those that eat longer strands also tend to eat macroalgae as well, but if the latter are abundant it hardly matters.

So the same checks as for cyanobacteria should be made and the same measures taken, except that antibiotics are of no use with algae. After correcting whatever is necessary so as to keep the problem to a minimum, introduce some algae-eaters. Fishes are the best first line of defense as they get around everywhere and can poke into places that molluscs may miss.

DINOFLAGELLATES

There used to be endless arguments among biologists about the nature of many of the organisms now classed as Protists, or Protoctista. Some claimed the dinoflagellates as plants, others as animals. Their inclusion in the new

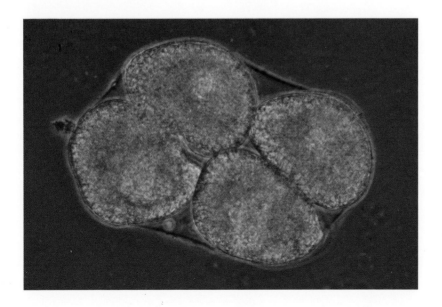

The organism causing saltwater velvet disease is a dinoflagellate, *Amyloodinium ocellatum*. Most dinoflagellates are free-living, however. Photo by Frickhinger.

kingdom puts an end to argument; they, together with protozoa, algae and slime moulds are all protists. Dinoflagellates are already familiar to aquarists as the cause of velvet disease in both fresh and salt water - *Oodinium* in fresh water and *Amyloodinium* in salt water. They are also the protists that live in the tissues of many corals and other invertebrates.

Corals that normally house the dinoflagellates, then known as zooxanthellae, rarely do well or even survive without them. In adverse conditions they expel the zooxanthellae and may never regain them.

Insufficient light, sudden changes in pH, specific gravity or just the general nature of the surrounding water can cause expulsion. This is one reason why large water changes, particularly with synthetic salts, are bad for reef tanks. Small, frequent changes do not alter the water enough to matter and should be preferred. If you are using natural sea water this precaution is less important as long as fairly frequent changes are made to keep the quality constant.

MACROALGAE

Many species of brown, red and especially green algae are kept in the

Halimeda species take calcium from sea water and deposit it in their cells, forming a hard structure similar to the skeleton of a coral. Over thousands of years their skeletons help produce reefs.

aquarium and will arise from living rock. They are decorative and help to take up nitrates and phosphates etc. from the water, but must be kept under control. Untended they may invade coral and kill off parts of the living rock by cutting out the light and smothering other inhabitants. This is particularly true of *Caulerpa*, which is very fast-growing and can reproduce from fragments. It also passes periodically into a reproductive phase, producing hair-like organs on the "leaves" and then dies off within a day or two. This pollutes the water unless speedy action is taken. Sudden changes in water quality are liable to stimulate the process, but it will happen sooner or later anyway.

For the reasons above, some aquarists avoid *Caulerpa* and stick to slower growing species. There are plenty available, other greens such as *Penicillus*, *Codium* and *Valonia*, browns such as *Padina* and *Dictyopterus* and reds like *Gracilaria* and *Gigortina*. Some, such as *Halimeda* (green) and the various coralline algae (reds) take up

calcium and become stony in character. These are important in nature and actually form more of a typical reef than the coral skeletons themselves, impacting between them and forming the solid reef. They cause no trouble but will only grow in an aquarium with water rich in calcium.

CALCIUM

The more you have in the way of stony corals and

Some green algae are wanted for their odd shapes. *Acetabularia*, with its spoked-wheel shape, is one of the more popular types. Photo by C. Platt.

155

algae, the greater the uptake of calcium from the water. Even the frequent small water changes usually recommended do not keep up with calcium loss in a typical reef tank. I experimented with a 6ft reef aquarium quite heavily populated with hard and soft corals but by no means as full of hard corals as it could have been. Starting with a normal calcium load of 400ppm (sea water is 410ppm) and with a 5% water change per week with natural sea water, the level of calcium fell in two months to 250ppm approximately. By this time the corals, both hard and soft, and various other inhabitants were looking decidedly less happy than usual. Most were not fully open or as active as normally. Replacement of the calcium over a week restored everything to normal. With many synthetic salts on the market, the loss rate would have been greater, since for some reason they are low in calcium to begin with.

Shortage of calcium in the reef aquarium must be common, since we have only quite recently discovered the need to use kalkwasser (lime water) or other methods of adding it on a regular basis. Strontium aids the uptake of calcium and is needed for optimal coral growth; without it the *Acropora* (staghorn) corals do not survive. It too must decline in the unsupplemented tank, although I have no way currently to measure it (sea water has 9ppm). I was still adding strontium to the tank mentioned above and this must have increased the rate of calcium loss. It may be necessary to add as much as several grams of calcium per day in a large aquarium. This means that unless evaporation is considerable, the addition of lime water may not be sufficient. Calcium chloride $(CaCl_2)$ is very soluble in water and so a 10% or 20% solution can be used to make up any deficiency.

Dilution of sea water may be good for some fishes and help to ward off diseases and parasites. It is not good in the reef tank. It lowers the calcium concentration as well as producing osmotic effects deleterious to many invertebrates. Even if the calcium is supplemented the second effect remains.

Suggested Reading

Shown here are just some of the books about marine fishes and invertebrates that have been published by T.F.H. Publications.

T.F.H. Publications is the world's largest publisher of books about pets of all kinds. TFH books should be available where you obtained this book; write to us for a free catalog of TFH books.

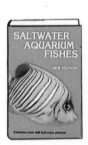

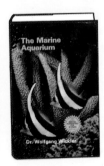

STARTING A
MARINE
AQUARIUM

MARINE
COMMUNITY
AQUARIUM

How Fish and Invertebrates Live Together
in the Miniature Reef Aquarium
By Dr. Leon P. Zann

Marine Aquariums

Three Full-Color Pull-Out Posters Inside

THE ABC'S OF
MARINE
AQUARIUMS
Dr. Warren E. Burgess

MARINE
AQUARIUMS
A COMPLETE INTRODUCTION

Dr. Warren E. Burgess

A STEP-BY-STEP BOOK ABOUT
TROPICAL MARINE
AQUARIUM FISHES
DR. C.W. EMMENS

exotic
marine fishes

MARINE
INVERTEBRATES

Marine Invertebrates
And Plants of the Living Reef

• Keys to identify reef invertebrates from the Gulf
  of Mexico, Caribbean Sea, Florida and the Tropical
  Atlantic.
• For the Miniature Reef Aquarium - SCUBA Diver -
  Snorkeler - Ichthyologist

ENCYCLOPEDIA
OF MARINE
INVERTEBRATES

EDITED BY
JERRY G. WALLS

the marine aquarium
in theory and practice
second edition, revised

MORE THAN 35 COLOR ILLUSTRATIONS
MARINE FISHES
AND
INVERTEBRATES
IN YOUR OWN HOME
By Dr. Cliff W. Emmens

A MINI-REEF IN YOUR OWN HOME.   FISH AND AQUARIUM MAINTENANCE.

INVERTEBRATES, CORALS AND PLANTS.   WHICH FISHES CAN LIVE TOGETHER.

fishes of southern japan
and the ryukyus
by dr. warren e. burgess & dr. herbert r. axelrod

pacific
marine
fishes
book 5

fishes of taiwan
and adjacent waters
by dr. herbert r. axelrod

fishes of the
great barrier reef
by warren e. burgess & dr. herbert r. axelrod

pacific
marine
fishes
book 7

CONTAINS MORE THAN 75 FULL-COLOR PHOTOGRAPHS
MARINE FISH
By Dr. Herbert R. Axelrod & Dr. Warren E. Burgess

MARINE AQUARIA
AND
MINIATURE REEFS
THE FISHES, THE INVERTEBRATES, THE TECHNIQUES

From choosing and using the
equipment right through picking the
best tankmates and detecting and
treating diseases—all by
the world's foremost authority on
miniature reef aquariums.

DR. C.W. EMMENS

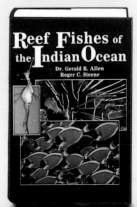

Reef Fishes of
the Indian Ocean
Dr. Gerald R. Allen
Roger C. Steene

INDEX

Page numbers in **boldface** refer to illustrations.